The Cherry Orchard

This translation of Chekhov's most famous comedy was originally published to coincide with Peter Hall's National Theatre production (1978) starring Dorothy Tutin, Albert Finney, Robert Stephens and Ralph Richardson. This revised version, with a new introduction and translation note, was published to coincide with Michael Codron's production at the Aldwych Theatre, London (1989) directed by Sam Mendes and starring Judi Dench, Ronald Pickup and Michael Gough.

ANTON CHEKHOV (1860–1904) first turned to writing as a medical student at Moscow University, from which he graduated in 1884. Among his early plays were short monologues (*The Evils of Tobacco*, 1885), one-act farces such as *The Bear*, *The Proposal* and *The Wedding* (1888–89) and the 'Platonov' material, adapted by Michael Frayn as *Wild Honey*. The first three full-length plays to be staged, *Ivanov* (1887), *The Wood Demon* (1889) and *The Seagull* (1896) were initially failures. But the Moscow Arts Theatre's revival of *The Seagull* two years later was successful and was followed by his master-pieces, *Uncle Vanya* (1889), *Three Sisters* (1901), and *The Cherry Orchard* in 1904, the year of his death.

Methuen's Theatre Classics

Anton Chekhov

THE CHERRY ORCHARD

A Comedy in Four Acts

Translated and introduced by
MICHAEL FRAYN

Methuen Drama

A METHUEN THEATRE CLASSIC

*This translation first published in Great Britain in 1978
as a paperback original by Eyre Methuen Ltd
Reprinted 1982, 1984 and 1986 by Methuen London Ltd
Reprinted in this revised edition 1988*

*Reprinted in 1990 by Methuen Drama,
an imprint of Reed Consumer Books Limited
Michelin House, 81 Fulham Road, London SW3 6RB
and Auckland, Melbourne, Singapore and Toronto
and distributed in the United States of America by Heinemann,
a division of Reed Publishing (USA) Inc.
361 Hanover Street, Portsmouth, New Hampshire NH 03801 3959
Reprinted in this revised edition 1990
Reprinted 1991 (twice), 1992 (three times), 1993*

*Translation opyright © 1978, 1988, 1990 by Michael Frayn
Introduction and chronology copyright © 1978, 1988, 1990 by
Michael Frayn*

*Printed in Great Britain by
Cox & Wyman Ltd., Reading, Berkshire*

ISBN 0 413 39340 2

*The front cover photograph shows Judi Dench as Ranyevskaya
and Michael Gough as Firs in Sam Mendes's 1989 Aldwych
production. The photograph of Chekhov on the back cover is
reproduced by courtesy of the Radio Times Hulton Picture
Library.*

Anton Pavlovich Chekhov

1860   Born the son of a grocer and grandson of a serf, in Taganrog, a small port on the Sea of Azov, where he spends his first nineteen years, and which he describes on a return visit in later life as 'Asia, pure and simple!'

1875   His father, bankrupt, flees from Taganrog concealed beneath a mat at the bottom of a cart.

1876   A former lodger buys the Chekhovs' house and puts the rest of the family out.

1879   Chekhov rejoins his family, who have followed his father to Moscow, and enrols at the university to study medicine.

1880   Begins contributing humorous material to minor magazines under the pen-name Antosha Chekhontc.

1882   Begins contributing regularly to the St Petersburg humorous journal *Oskolki* – short stories and sketches, and a column on Moscow life.

1884   Qualifies as a doctor, and begins practising in Moscow – the start of a sporadic second career which over the years brings him much hard work but little income.

1885   Begins writing for the *St Petersburg Gazette*, which gives him the opportunity to break out of the tight restrictions on length and the rigidly humorous format in which he has worked up to now.

1886   Another step up the journalistic ladder – he begins writing, under his own name and for good money, for *Novoye vremya*. Alexei Suvorin, its millionaire proprietor, an anti-Semitic reactionary who had the concession on all the railway bookstands in Russia, becomes Chekhov's close friend.

1887   Is a literary success in St Petersburg. Writes *Ivanov* as a result of a commission from a producer who wants a light entertainment in the Chekhonte style. The play is produced in Moscow (his first production) to a mixture of clapping and hissing.

1888   Begins to publish his stories in the 'thick journals'; has survived his career in comic journalism to emerge as a serious and respectable writer. But at the same time begins writing four one-act farces for the theatre.

1889   *The Wood Demon* (which Chekhov later uses as raw material for *Uncle Vanya*) opens at a second-rate Moscow theatre, and survives for only three performances.

1890 Makes the appalling journey across Siberia (largely in unsprung carts over unsurfaced roads) to visit and report on the penal colony on the island of Sakhalin. Sets out to interview the entire population of prisoners and exiles, at the rate of 160 a day.

1892 Travels the back country of Nizhny Novgorod and Voronyezh provinces in the middle of winter, trying to prevent a recurrence of the previous year's famine among the peasants. Is banqueted by the provincial governors. Moves to the modest but comfortable estate he had bought himself at Melikhovo, fifty miles south of Moscow. Becomes an energetic and enlightened landowner, cultivating the soil and doctoring the peasants. Spends three months organizing the district against an expected cholera epidemic.

1894 Starts work on the first of the three schools he builds in the Melikhovo district.

1896 *The Seagull* opens in St Petersburg, and survives only five performances after a disastrous first night. Chekhov tells Suvorin he won't have another play put on even if he lives another seven hundred years.

1897 Suffers a violent lung haemorrhage while dining with Suvorin, and is forced to recognize at last what he has long closed his eyes to – that he is suffering from advanced consumption. (Is also constantly plagued by piles, gastritis, migraine, dizzy spells, and palpitations of the heart.) Winters in Nice.

1898 Moves his headquarters to the Crimean warmth of Yalta. Stanislavsky revives *The Seagull* (with twelve weeks rehearsal) at the newly-founded Moscow Arts Theatre, and it is an immediate success.

1899 Sells the copyright in all his works, past, present, and future, to the St Petersburg publisher A. F. Marks – a contract which is to burden the rest of his life. *Uncle Vanya* produced successfully by the Moscow Arts Theatre.

1901 *Three Sisters* produced by the Moscow Arts Theatre, but rather poorly received. Chekhov marries his mistress, Olga Knipper, an actress in the Moscow Arts company, the original Arkadina in *The Seagull*, Yelena in *Uncle Vanya*, Masha in *Three Sisters* and Ranyevskaya in *The Cherry Orchard*.

1904 *The Cherry Orchard* is produced in January; and in July, after two heart attacks, Chekhov dies in a hotel bedroom in the German spa of Badenweiler.

Introduction

By the time Chekhov came to write *The Cherry Orchard*, in 1903, he was dying. This final play gave him one of the hardest struggles he had ever had. His tuberculosis left him increasingly exhausted, while his waning strength was further eroded by the discomfort of his life in Yalta, and by travelling back and forth to Moscow because of disagreement between his doctors about which climate would suit him best. There was tension in the household, too, between his sister, Masha, and his new wife, Olga Knipper; while the short hours of his working day were wasted by the perpetual stream of visitors that his fame attracted. In the end the play was a triumph, and at the first performance, on 17 January 1904, his forty-fourth birthday, he was brought up on stage between acts three and four for lengthy speeches and presentations. But by this time he was visibly failing; he had only another four months to live.

It was the play itself that presented the greatest problems. He had been thinking about it for two years before he began to write, and it had been conceived from the very first as a comedy. 'The next play that I write,' he said in a letter to Knipper in March, 1901, 'will definitely be a funny one, a very funny one, at any rate in conception.' In another letter he described it as 'a four-act vaudeville,' and in the autumn of that year, according to Stanislavsky, he gave the actors at the Moscow Arts a kind of oral trailer for what he had in mind. Three of the four disconnected details he produced were essentially comic: a servant who went fishing; a cheerful billiards enthusiast with a loud voice and only one arm; and the owner (male or female) of a country estate who kept borrowing money off the servant. This list may have been more in the nature of a whimsical camouflage for his intentions than a serious exposition of them – it would have been very much his style. He may even have been joking when he included as the fourth item an even smaller and more disconnected detail: 'a branch of cherry blossom sticking out of the garden straight into the room through an open window.'

From this one tiny visual flourish, however, came the real play – and all his difficulties with accommodating it to his original comic conception. During the course of the next two years he must have traced that branch back out of the window – back to the orchard in which the tree was rooted, back to the social history and economic forces which explained why that orchard had been planted and why it was now about to be felled. The trail took him not only outwards through Russian society and across the Russian landscape, but backwards in time through his own writing and his own life. From where he now stood, on the brink of his last work, and at the end of his life, he found himself returning to themes he had touched upon in his stories over his entire professional career, and going back further still, to his childhood. As a schoolboy in Taganrog he had heard stories told by the mother of one of his friends about her life as a landowner before the Emancipation (on an estate where there was an ancient serf like Firs) in Poltava province, which was famous for its cherry orchards. He had spent summer holidays as a child on a rural estate out in the steppe to the north of Taganrog, where his grandfather (a manumitted serf himself) was steward. He had heard the distant sound of a breaking cable in the mines while he was staying with a boyhood friend on another property in the steppe. His own modest family home had been sold off to pay his father's debts – and bought by the wealthy friend who had promised to save it. By the time he began to write the play, that single branch at the window had led him to a world which was remarkably difficult to accommodate in a 'four-act vaudeville'.

In fact *The Cherry Orchard* is the most elusive and difficult of all these four last plays. There are not only the mysteries that all his other late plays contain. (Why has Ranyevskaya adopted Varya? There is no mention of her background or parentage. Is she known – to everyone but us – to be the illegitimate daughter of Ranyevskaya's drunken late husband?) The whole approach has become noticeably less naturalistic, and more dependent upon mood and symbolism. (Chekhov may have been planning to go further in this direction with the extraordinary new departure he was contemplating at the time of his death – a play about Arctic exploration.) It is also even less directly dramatic. The conflict from which the play springs is intense; the Gayev family is being broken apart by powerful forces – forces rooted deep in history and in the society around them. But in the whole course of the play only one dramatic event is thrown up by this conflict – the crisis itself, the announcement by Lopakhin that he has bought the estate. There is a curious air of detachment about some of the episodes. Charlotta Ivanovna's musing about her past, and the irruption of the Passer-by, seem like side-eddies at the edge of the main river. For the whole of this second act, in fact, the narrative comes to a halt. Life hangs suspended for a while in the old mode before everything finally changes, like water scarcely moving in the depths of the millpool before it plunges down the race to the wheel.

Chekhov confessed to Knipper that he had been 'scared' himself by the 'lack of movement' in Act Two. So was Stanislavsky when he saw it in rehearsal. 'For a long time the play was not working,' he wrote later. 'Particularly the second act. It contains no action, in the theatrical sense, and at rehearsals seemed very monotonous. It was essential to show the boredom of doing nothing in a way that was interesting.' He asked for cuts. Chekhov did more than cut; he rearranged and rewrote. (The material that came out can be found in A Note on the Translation.) The cuts were restored in Mike Alfreds's production of the play at the National Theatre, but this seems to me quite wrong. The alterations went into the original production only a month after it had opened when it was already an established success. It is difficult to believe that Chekhov would have made them at that stage if he had not fully concurred in them himself. But they shed a little more light on several of the characters. Charlotta Ivanovna has a good line about Ranyevskaya – 'She's perpetually mislaying things. She's mislaid her life, even.' And Firs is more plainly seen as what he is – a peasant, an ex-serf, rather than a kind of Russian Jeeves.

Two other characters have in the past been much misunderstood by directors. Natural sympathy for the Gayev family and their feckless charm has sometimes obscured the qualities of

Lopakhin and Trofimov, the representatives of economic and political progress who are, in their different ways, pushing them to the margins of life. ('Suddenly no one needs us any more,' as Gayev sadly discovers in Act Four, when the money has gone.) They both feel genuine love for their unintended victims, and Chekhov's letters make it clear that he took a characteristically objective view of both of them. 'Lopakhin is a businessman, it's true,' he wrote to Stanislavsky, conscious of the way in which progressive prejudice was likely to work, 'but he is in every sense a decent person. He must behave with complete decorum and propriety, without pettiness or trickery . . . In casting this part it must be kept in mind that Lopakhin has been loved by Varya, a serious and religious young lady; she wouldn't have fallen in love with some grasping peasant.'

Trofimov has suffered in different ways. In the past he has sometimes been portrayed in English productions as an inadequate and immature personality who is afraid to emerge from university and face the real world. This view has been given currency by the translation which has become traditional for his ironic description of himself – 'the eternal student', a phrase that suggests in English not only the correct primary meaning of remaining a student forever, but also (as in 'the eternal schoolboy' or 'the eternal triangle') the idea of his being the unchanging student *type*. The Russian phrase, *vyechniy studyent*, has quite a different overtone; it is a variant of *vyechniy zhid*, literally 'the eternal Jew', but in English the Wandering Jew, who was condemned to wander the earth for all eternity without shelter. Chekhov makes the implication of this clear in the same letter to Knipper in which he admits to his worries about Act Two. His other anxiety, he says, is '. . . the somewhat unfinished state of the student, Trofimov. The point is that Trofimov is perpetually being exiled, perpetually being thrown out of the university – and how do you show things like this?' Exiled, of course, for his political activities; and the difficulty of showing things like this being the censor (who, even as it was, cut two passages from Trofimov's speeches – about the condition of the workers and about the effect that the ownership of serfs has had upon the Gayev family). Chekhov plainly takes Trofimov seriously as a man who holds sane and genuine convictions for which he is prepared to suffer. But then to go to the opposite extreme, as was done in Trevor Griffiths's adaptation of the play, and to turn him into a 'positive hero' in the Socialist Realist sense, is also an absurdity. Even if we had not discovered by now that Chekhov's characters are never puppets, Trofimov and his beliefs, like Vershinin and his, are obviously being held at some slight ironic distance. He is plainly ridiculous when he claims to be 'above such things as love'. Even his sincerest speeches topple into rhetoric about mankind marching towards higher truth and higher happiness. (His excited outburst to Anya at the end of Act Two – 'On, on, on! We are going to that bright star that blazes from afar there, and no one can hold us back! On, on, on! In step together, friends!' – echoes a famous revolutionary ode by Pleshcheyev, the writer to whom Chekhov addressed his disclaimer of all political and religious enthusiasm – 'On, on, with neither fear nor doubting/To great and valorous feats, my friends . . .!/And like a guiding star on high/Let blaze for us the sacred truth . . .'). He complains about people doing nothing but talk even as he stands there doing nothing but talk. Lopakhin and Trofimov, in fact, like all Chekhov's characters, speak out boldly and sincerely in their own voices. Each rises to his heights of magnanimity and understanding, and each comes up against his own particular limitations.

The greatest problem, though, in playing and understanding *The Cherry Orchard* is to know whether or not it is a comedy. Are we to laugh or are we to cry? Both, no doubt. But this is easier to achieve in theory than in practice, and on the page rather than on the stage. An audience is a large, corporate creature with large, corporate emotions. It can stand close to the sufferer and feel his pain, or it can hold him at arm's length and see the absurdity of his helplessness; it finds it very difficult to be in both places at once. The ambiguity of the text gives the people who have to perform it genuine practical difficulties, and they must always be tempted to resolve them by pushing the tone in one direction or the other.

The same problem arises with all the last four plays, and is likely to go on puzzling directors and actors, not to mention translators, as long as they are performed. But it becomes particularly acute in *The Cherry Orchard*. Chekhov went on insisting that it was a 'vaudeville', even after the material had changed out of all recognition in the writing. He designates it a comedy on the title-page, and in his letters he said it was 'not a drama but a comedy, in places even a farce . . .'. 'The last act will be cheerful – in fact the whole play will be cheerful and frivolous . . .'. He was not using these terms in some arcane private sense; the short plays that he wrote earlier in his life are after all quite unambiguously cheerful and frivolous, quite straightforwardly comedies, farces, and vaudevilles.

Stanislavsky's reaction to all this was to tell Chekhov bluntly that he was wrong. 'It's not a comedy, it's not a farce, as you wrote,' he informed him, after everyone had wept in the last act during the read-through at the Moscow Arts, 'it's a tragedy . . . I wept like a woman. I tried to stop myself, but I couldn't. I can hear you saying, "Excuse me, but it is in fact a farce . . .". No, for the plain man it is a tragedy.'

In the past most directors seem to have agreed with Stanislavsky. More recently the pendulum has swung the opposite way, and it has become fashionable to establish the comic nature of all these four plays by presenting the characters as ludicrously self-obsessed grotesques, and by supplying sight-gags that the author overlooked. This may be another example of the somewhat eccentric influence exercised by David Magarshack, one of the most distinguished of Chekhov's translators. In his book *Chekhov the Dramatist* he urges the view that *The Cherry Orchard* is simply a funny play in its entirety. He even manages to find the last scene funny, where Firs is left locked into the empty house for the winter. He argues that the stage-direction says merely that Firs is lying motionless, not dying, and that someone will shortly realise what has happened, and come back and release him. This seems to me frankly preposterous. No doubt Firs is not clinically dead at the fall of the curtain, but anyone who believes he has a serious chance of emerging from that room alive has clearly never considered the practicalities of play-writing, let alone the effects of extreme cold upon extreme old age. In the course of the last act Chekhov establishes not once but three times, in a brilliantly escalating confirmation of misunderstanding, that the family believes Firs to have been taken off to hospital already; not once but four times that the house is to be closed up for the winter; and even twice that the temperature is already three degrees below zero. If you can believe that after all this there remained in Chekhov's mind some unexpressed hope that Gayev, say, might get the next train back from town, or that Yepikhodov might for some reason suddenly take it into his head to unlock the house again and inspect its contents, then you can believe that Wagner hoped the local fire brigade might just get there in time at the end of *Götterdämmerung*.

Nor will the text as a whole support Magarshack's view. As in all the plays, something is being lost – something that will never be recovered even if all the bright prophecies of the optimists were to come true tomorrow. Those trees, that begin in blossom and end beneath the axe, are everything that ever can be lost by mortal man – childhood, happiness, purpose, love, and all the brightness of life. It is truly not possible to read the play in Russian without being moved, as Stanislavsky and his company were, to tears as well as to laughter.

Some of Chekhov's references to the play's comicality have a characteristically teasing or self-mocking air – he was deeply shocked when Stanislavsky was said to be thinking of staging one of his actual vaudevilles at the Arts Theatre. He was also engaged in a running battle with Stanislavsky over the ponderousness of his staging. With *The Cherry Orchard* he evidently feared the worst from the very beginning. 'I should very much like to be around at rehearsals to have a look,' he wrote anxiously to Nemirovich-Danchenko. 'I am afraid that Anya might have a tearful tone of voice (you for some reason find her similar to Irina) . . . Not once in my text does Anya weep, and nowhere does she speak in a tearful voice. In the second act she has tears in her eyes, but her tone of voice is cheerful and lively. Why in your telegram do you talk about there being a lot of people weeping in the play? Where are they? The only one is Varya, but that's because Varya is a crybaby by nature, and her tears are not supposed to elicit a feeling of gloom in the audience. In my text it often says "on the verge of tears", but that indicates merely the characters' mood, not tears. There is no cemetery in the second act.'

But even these quite specific comments can't be taken too literally, because they are at variance with Chekhov's own text. According to the stage-directions, Gayev is 'wiping away his tears' in Act Three. Ranyevskaya, at the end of the act, is 'weeping bitterly'. Both of them, at the end of the last act, 'sob quietly'. Part of what Chekhov wanted when he insisted on the comedy in his plays was surely a different style of playing; he was looking for lightness, speed, indifference, and irony; something that suggested not the inexorable tolling of fate but the absurdity of human intentions and the meaninglessness of events.

The Cherry Orchard, though, does seem to me to be a comedy in some sense that the other plays are not, and I think it is possible to grasp this aspect of it without losing sight of its painfulness; indeed, to see the suffering of the characters as being expressed through the comic inappropriateness of their reactions. The slothful reluctance of the Gayevs to face what is happening to them, their inability to save the ship by jettisoning the cargo, is undoubtedly comic. And Chekhov is right about the last act; it is in some sense cheerful. The crisis has occurred at the end of Act Three, as it does in *Uncle Vanya*. What it calls forth in the characters, however, is not a spirit of endurance, as it does in the earlier play, but the absurd lightening of the spirits that occurs, as Chekhov has observed with the most wonderful ironic shrewdness, after a decision has been taken, however terrible, and the worst has actually happened. It is notable that in this last play, with his own death only months away, Chekhov is struck not so much by the inexorable nature of terrible events as by their survivability, by their way of slipping out of the mind, once they have occurred, and of disappearing in the endless wash of further events.

But the cheerfulness is deeply poignant. The worst *has* happened, and it is a bad worst. The Gayevs' happiness has been irretrievably lost, as both brother and sister for one moment realise before they leave the house; and their future will be even bleaker than Nina's on her tours of second-rate provincial theatres, or Vanya's and Sonya's at the account-books of their provincial estate, or the Prozorov sisters' in their grim northern exile. A few months work at the bank for Gayev; a few months with her hopeless lover in Paris for Ranyevskaya. Then resolution and love and the last of the money will all run out. They will have neither home nor occupation; nothing. There is something absurd about their prospects, though, because the Gayevs remain too feckless to understand them; they lack the tragic dignity that Sonya and her uncle and the Prozorov sisters all muster in the end. This is why, finally, the play is a comedy. It is the comedy of inertia and helplessness in the face of truly desolating loss. There is no simple formula for playing it, or for responding to it; the problem it sets us is the problem of life itself.

MICHAEL FRAYN

A Note on the Translation

Although this is Chekhov's last play it was the first one I translated (it was commissioned for Peter Hall's production at the National Theatre in 1978). By the time it was revived in London, for the production by Sam Mendes at the Aldwych Theatre in 1989, I had discovered a little more about translating Chekhov, and I made a fair number of revisions.

I have, as always, been fairly ruthless about names. I have teased out *vyechniy studyent* (see Introduction), and attached a date to the emancipation of the serfs, which would have been as firmly located in Russian minds as (say) the Second World War in ours. I have supplied what Chekhov merely specifies in a stage-direction, the first few lines of Alexei Tolstoy's marvellously bad poem *The Scarlet Woman*, which is about a Judean courtesan who boasts that she will subdue Jesus with one of her irresistible looks, and instead is herself subdued by John the Baptist with one of his.

I am still in two minds about the scene with the Passer-by. In the original, after the words 'Wonderful weather', he 'declaims' a few words. Baldly translated they are meaningless: 'My brother, my suffering brother . . . go out to the Volga; whose groans . . .?' In fact the line consists of two quotations (or misquotations). The first half is taken from an indifferent poem by Nadson, whom I suspect, from references in the letters, Chekhov despised. The second half comes from what seems to me a rather magnificent poem by Nekrasov, *Reflections on the Gateway to a Great House*. I have supplied enough of each poem to make sense – and the sense parallels a lot of Trofimov's ideas. This makes the Passer-by's 'declamation' into rather a performance, whereas in the original he is behaving like carol-singers who give you two lines of *Hark the Herald Angel Sings*, then hold out their hand for money. I have left my extended version in the text for anyone who wants it, but on balance I think it would be better to cut it, and go straight from 'Wonderful weather' to 'Mademoiselle, spare a few kopeks for a starving Russian'.

It may, incidentally, be relevant in understanding this scene that the word for 'Passer-by', *prokhozhy*, meant in Siberian usage at that time someone who was tramping the roads to escape from prison or exile. Chekhov must have come across this usage on his journey to Sakhalin, though whether he intended any part of that sense here I do not know.

Before Chekhov rewrote Act Two after the opening in Moscow (see Introduction) Charlotta did not appear in the scene at the beginning of the act, and Trofimov did not have his two speeches at the end, where he asks Anya to have faith in him, and sees happiness coming with the rising moon. Instead the act began with a scene between Trofimov and Anya:

> YASHA *and* DUNYASHA *are sitting on the bench.* YEPIKHODOV *is standing beside it.* TROFIMOV *and* ANYA *come along the path from the estate.*

ANYA. Great-aunt is all alone in the world – she's very wealthy. She's no love for Mama. The first few days I was there I found it very hard – she didn't say much to me. Then she cheered up and started to laugh. She promised to send the money – she gave me and Charlotta some for the journey. Oh, but it's a horrible feeling, being the poor relation.

TROFIMOV. It now looks as if there's someone here already . . . Sitting on the bench. Let's go on, then.

ANYA. I was away from home for three weeks. I started to pine most dreadfully.

> TROFIMOV *and* ANYA *go out.*

Then Dunyasha says 'All the same, how lovely to spend some time abroad . . .' After Ranyevskaya's line, 'Perhaps we'll think of something,' the original text continued:

> VARYA *and* CHARLOTTA IVANOVNA *come along the path from the estate.* CHARLOTTA *is wearing a man's suit, and is carrying a gun.*

VARYA. She's a sensible, well-brought-up girl, and nothing can happen, but all the same she shouldn't be left alone with a young man. Supper at nine o'clock. Make sure you're not late.

CHARLOTTA. I'm not hungry. (*Hums quietly.*)

VARYA. It doesn't matter. You must be there for appearances' sake. Look, they're sitting over there, on the bank.

VARYA *and* CHARLOTTA IVANOVNA *go out.*

And at the end of the act, after Anya's line: 'You put it so beautifully!' the scene originally continued:

TROFIMOV. Sh . . . Someone's coming. It's that Varya again! (*Angrily.*) It's outrageous!

ANYA. Come on – let's go down to the river. It's nice there.

TROFIMOV. Come on, then.

ANYA. The moon will be rising soon.

ANYA *and* TROFIMOV *go out.*

Enter FIRS, *then* CHARLOTTA IVANOVNA. FIRS *mutters away as he looks for something on the ground near the bench. He strikes a match.*

FIRS. Oh, you sillybilly!

CHARLOTTA (*sits down on the bench and takes off her peaked cap*). Is that you, Firs? What are you looking for?

FIRS. The mistress has lost her purse.

CHARLOTTA (*searches*). Here's her fan. And here's her hand-kerchief – it smells of perfume. (*Pause.*) There isn't anything else. She's perpetually mislaying things. She's mislaid her life, even. (*Hums quietly.*) I haven't got proper papers – I don't know how old I am. So I think of myself as being young . . . (*Puts the cap on* FIRS, *who sits motionless.*) Oh, I love you, my dear sir! (*Laughs.*) *Ein, zwei, drei!* (*Takes the cap off* FIRS, *and puts it on herself.*) When I was a little girl, Mama and my father used to go round all the fairs . . .

And she gives what is now the opening speech of the act, down to, 'I don't know anything.' Then:

FIRS. When I was twenty, twenty-five years old, I was going along one day with the deacon's son and the cook, Vasily, and

just here, on this stone, there was a man sitting . . . a stranger –
belonged to someone else – we didn't know him . . . For some
reason I got scared, and I went off, and after I'd gone the other
two set on him and killed him . . . He'd got money on him.

CHARLOTTA. So? *Weiter!* Go on!

FIRS. So then along came the law, and they started to question us.
They took the pair of them away . . . they took me, too. I was
two years in jail . . . Then that was that, they let us go. It was a
long while back. (*Pause.*) I can't remember it all.

CHARLOTTA. An old man like you – it's time for you to die.
(*Eats the cucumber.*)

FIRS. Eh? (*Mutters to himself.*) So there they were, they all went
along together, and there they stopped . . . Uncle jumped down
from the cart . . . he picked up the sack . . . and inside that
sack was another sack. And he looks, and there's something
going twitch! twitch!

CHARLOTTA (*laughs quietly*). Twitch, twitch! (*Eats the cucumber.*)

*Someone can be heard walking quietly along the path and quietly
playing the balalaika. The moon rises. Somewhere over by the
poplars* VARYA *is looking for* ANYA.

VARYA (*calling, off*). Anya! Where are you?

Curtain.

The Pronunciation of the Names

The following is an approximate practical guide. In general, all stressed a's are pronounced as in 'far' (the sound is indicated below by 'aa') and all stressed o's as in 'more' (they are written below as 'aw'). All unstressed a's and o's are thrown away and slurred. The u's are pronounced as in 'crude'; they are shown below as 'oo'.

Ranyevskaya (Lyuba, Lyubov Andreyevna) – Ran*yev*skaya
  (*Lyoob*a, Lyoob*awf* And*ray*evna)
Anya, Anyechka – *Aan*ya, *Aan*yechka
Varya – *Vaar*ya
Gayev (Leonid Andreyich, Lenya) –
  Guy-(as in Fawkes)-yev, *Len*ya, Leo*need* And*ray*ich)
Lopakhin (Yermolay) – Lo*paakh*een (Yermo*lie* – as in 'lie'
  meaning 'untruth')
Trofimov (Petya) – Tro*feem*ov (*Pet*ya)
Simeonov-Pishchik – Sim*yawn*ov-*Peesh*-cheek
Charlotta Ivanovna – Shar*lawt*a Eev*aan*ovna
Yepikhodov – Yepi*khawd*ov
Dunyasha – Doon*yaash*a
Firs – Fierce
Yasha – *Yaash*a

Anastasy – Ana*staas*y
Dashenka – *Daash*enka
Deriganov – Deri*gaan*ov
Grisha – *Greesh*a
Kardamonov – Karda*mawn*ov
Karp – Kaarp
Kharkov – *Khaar*kov

Kozoyedov (Fyodor) – Kozoyedov (*Fyaw* – dor – two
   syllables, not three)
Lopakhina – Lo*paakh*ina
Mama – *Maam*a
Petrushka – Pe*troosh*ka
Polya – *Pawl*ya
Ragulin – Rag*ool*in
Tolstoy (Aleksey Konstantinovich) – Tol*stoy* (Alek*say*
   Konstan*teen*ovich)
Yaroslavl – Yaros*laavl*
Yashnevo – *Yaash*nevo
Yefimushka – Ye*feem*ooshka
Yegor – Ye*gawr*
Yevstigney – Yevstig*nay*
Znoykov – *Znoy*kov

This translation of The Cherry Orchard *was first staged by the National Theatre in the Olivier on 3 February 1978. The cast was as follows:*

RANYEVSKAYA *(Lyuba), a landowner*	Dorothy Tutin
ANYA, *her daughter, aged 17*	Judi Bowker
VARYA, *her adopted daughter, aged 24*	Susan Fleetwood
GAYEV *(Lenya), Ranyevskaya's brother*	Robert Stephens
LOPAKHIN *(Yermolay), a businessman*	Albert Finney
TROFIMOV *(Pyetya), a student*	Ben Kingsley
SIMEONOV-PISHCHIK, *a landowner*	Terence Rigby
CHARLOTTA IVANOVNA, *the governess*	Helen Ryan
YEPIKHODOV, *the estate clerk*	Nicky Henson
DUNYASHA, *the chambermaid*	Susan Littler
FIRS, *the footman, an old man of 87*	Ralph Richardson
YASHA, *the young footman*	Derek Thompson
A PASSER-BY	Peter Needham
THE STATIONMASTER	Daniel Thorndike

Directed by Peter Hall
Designed by John Bury

The action takes place on Ranyevskaya's estate.

This revised translation of The Cherry Orchard *was produced by Michael Codron and staged at the Aldwych Theatre, London on 24 October 1989, with the following cast:*

DUNYASHA, *the chambermaid*	Abigail McKern
LOPAKHIN (Yermola), *a businessman*	Bernard Hill
YEPIKHODOV, *the estate clerk*	Tom Watt
FIRS, *the footman*	Michael Gough
ANYA, *Ranyevskaya's daughter*	Miranda Foster
RANYEVSKAYA (Lyuba), *a landowner*	Judi Dench
CHARLOTTA IVANOVNA, *the governess*	Kate Duchêne
VARYA, *Ranyevskaya's adopted daughter*	Lesley Manville
GAYEV (Lenya), *Ranyevskaya's brother*	Ronald Pickup
SIMEONOV-PISCHIK, *a landowner*	Barry Stanton
YASHA, *the young footman*	John Dougall
TROFIMOV (Petya), *a student*	Nicholas Farrell
A PASSER-BY	Tom Hollander
THE STATIONMASTER	Stanley Page
THE POSTMASTER	Peter Sowerbutts
PARTY GUESTS	Kate Anthony
	Patricia Samuels

Directed by Sam Mendes
Designed by Paul Farnworth

Act One

A room which is still known as the nursery. One of the doors leads to ANYA's *room. Half-light, shortly before sunrise. It is May already, and the cherry trees are in blossom, but outside in the orchard it is cold, with a morning frost. The windows are closed.*

Enter DUNYASHA *with a candle, and* LOPAKHIN *with a book in his hand.*

LOPAKHIN. God be praised, the train's arrived. What time is it?

DUNYASHA. Nearly two o'clock. (*Extinguishes the candle.*) It's light already.

LOPAKHIN. So the train's how late? Two hours, at least. (*Yawns and stretches.*) Fine one I am. Complete fool. Came all the way here to go and meet them at the station, and then just dropped off while I was sitting there. It's a shame. You might have woken me.

DUNYASHA. I thought you'd gone. (*Listens.*) That sounds like them now.

LOPAKHIN (*listens*). No . . . Luggage to pick up, one thing and another . . .

Pause.

She's lived abroad for five years – I don't know what she'll be like now . . . She's a fine woman. Easy, straightforward. I remember, when I was a boy of fifteen or so, my father – he kept a shop then in the village here – dead now, of course – he punched me in the face, and the blood started to pour out of my nose . . . For some reason we'd come into the yard here together, and he was drunk. It seems like yesterday. She was only young – such a slim young thing. She brought me in and she took me to the washstand in this room, in the nursery.

'Don't cry, my little peasant,' she says. 'It'll heal in time for your wedding . . .'

Pause.

My little peasant . . . it's true, my father was a peasant – and here am I in a white waistcoat and yellow shoes. Like a pig in a pastry-cook's . . . The only difference is I'm a rich man, plenty of money, but look twice and I'm a peasant, a real peasant . . . (*Leafs through the book.*) I was reading this book. Couldn't understand a word. Fell asleep over it.

Pause.

DUNYASHA. And the dogs, they haven't slept all night. They can sense that the mistress is coming.

LOPAKHIN. What's the matter with you, Dunyasha?

DUNYASHA. My hands are all of a tremble. I'm going to faint.

LOPAKHIN. Very tender plant, aren't you, Dunyasha? Dress like a lady, do your hair like one, too. Not the way, is it? You want to remember who you are.

Enter YEPIKHODOV *with a bouquet. He is wearing a jacket and highly polished boots that squeak loudly. As he comes in he drops the bouquet.*

YEPIKHODOV (*picks up the bouquet*). The gardener sent them. He says to put them in the dining-room. (*Gives the bouquet to* DUNYASHA.)

LOPAKHIN. And bring me some kvass.

DUNYASHA. Very good. (*Goes out.*)

YEPIKHODOV. Three degrees of frost this morning, and the cherry all in blossom. I can't give our climate my seal of approval. (*Sighs.*) Indeed I can't. It never knows how to lend a helping hand at the right moment. And I mean look at me – I bought myself these boots the day before yesterday, and they squeak so much, I mean it's quite impossible. I mean, put it like this – what should I grease them with?

LOPAKHIN. Leave off, will you? Pester, pester.

YEPIKHODOV. I don't know. Every day some disaster happens to me. Not that I complain. I'm used to it. I even smile.

Enter DUNYASHA. *She gives* LOPAKHIN *his kvass.*

YEPIKHODOV. I'll go, then. (*Stumbles against the table, which falls over.*) There you are ... (*As if exulting in it.*) You see what I'm up against! I mean, it's simply amazing! (*Goes out.*)

DUNYASHA. To tell you the truth, he's proposed to me.

LOPAKHIN. Ah!

DUNYASHA. I don't know *what* to say ... He's all right, he doesn't give any trouble, it's just sometimes when he starts to talk – you can't understand a word of it. It's very nice, and he puts a lot of feeling into it, only you can't understand it. I quite like him in a way, even. He's madly in love with me. He's the kind of person who never has any luck. Every day something happens. They tease him in our part of the house – they call him Disasters by the Dozen ...

LOPAKHIN (*listens*). I think they're coming.

DUNYASHA. They're coming! What's the matter with me? I've gone all cold.

LOPAKHIN. They are indeed coming. Let's go and meet them. Will she recognize me? Five years we haven't seen each other.

DUNYASHA (*in agitation*). I'll faint this very minute ... I will, I'll faint clean away!

Two carriages can be heard coming up to the house. LOPAKHIN *and* DUNYASHA *hurry out.*

The stage is empty. Then there is noise in the adjoining rooms. Across the stage, leaning on his stick, hurries FIRS, *who has gone to the station to meet the mistress. He is wearing ancient livery and a top hat. He is saying something to himself, but not a word of it can be made out. The noise offstage grows louder and louder.*

A VOICE (*off*). This way, look.

> *Enter* RANYEVSKAYA, ANYA, *and* CHARLOTTA IVANOVNA, *who has a little dog on a lead. All three ladies are dressed for travelling:* VARYA *in an overcoat and shawl;* GAYEV, SIMEONOV-PISHCHIK, LOPAKHIN, DUNYASHA *with a bundle and an umbrella,* SERVANTS *carrying things – they all go across the room.*

ANYA. This way. Mama, do you remember which room this is?

RANYEVSKAYA (*joyfully, on the verge of tears*). The nursery!

VARYA. So cold. My hands are quite numb. (*To* RANYEVSKAYA.) Your rooms – the white one and the mauve one – they've stayed just as they were, Mama.

RANYEVSKAYA. The nursery. My own dear room, my lovely room . . . I slept in here when I was a little girl. (*Weeps.*) And now I'm like a little girl again . . . (*Kisses her brother, then* VARYA, *then her brother once more.*) And Varya's just the same as before – she looks like a nun. And Dunyasha I recognize . . . (*Kisses her.*)

GAYEV. The train was two hours late. What do you think of that? What kind of standards do these people have?

CHARLOTTA (*to* PISHCHIK). My dog can eat nuts even.

PISHCHIK (*surprised*). Would you believe it!

> *They all go out except* ANYA *and* DUNYASHA.

DUNYASHA. We waited and waited . . . (*She takes off* ANYA'S *coat and hat.*)

ANYA. I didn't sleep on the way – I haven't slept for four nights . . . Oh, I'm completely frozen!

DUNYASHA. You went away in Lent, with snow on the ground still, and now look at it. Oh, my dear! (*Laughs and kisses her.*) I've waited and waited for you. My own precious! My heart's delight . . .! I'm going to tell you at once – I can't contain myself another minute . . .

ANYA (*inertly*). Nothing else.

DUNYASHA. Yepikhodov – you know who I mean, the estate clerk – just after Easter he proposed to me.

ANYA. Still on about the same old thing . . . (*Tidying her hair.*) I've gradually lost all the pins . . .

She is completely exhausted – unable to keep her balance, even.

DUNYASHA. I don't know *what* to think. He's in love with me, so in love with me!

ANYA (*looks into her room, tenderly*). My room, my windows, just as if I'd never been away. I'll get up in the morning, I'll run out into the orchard . . . Oh, if only I could get to sleep! I didn't sleep all the way – I was worn out with worry.

DUNYASHA. The day before yesterday Mr. Trofimov arrived.

ANYA (*joyfully*). Petya!

DUNYASHA. He's sleeping in the bath-house – he's living out there. He said he was afraid of being in the way. (*Looks at her pocket watch.*) We ought to wake him up, but Miss Varya said not to. Don't you go waking him, she says.

Enter VARYA, with a bunch of keys on her belt.

VARYA. Dunyasha, quick now – Mama's asking for coffee.

DUNYASHA. Very good. (*Goes out.*)

VARYA. Well, God be praised, you've got here, both of you. You're home again, Anya. (*Cuddling her.*) My darling's come home! My lovely's come home again!

ANYA. I've had a most terrible time.

VARYA. I can imagine.

ANYA. I set out from here in Holy Week. It was cold. Charlotta talked the whole way – she kept showing me conjuring tricks. Why on earth you saddled me with Charlotta . . .

VARYA. You couldn't have travelled alone, my darling. Not at seventeen!

ANYA. Anyway, we get to Paris, and it's cold, it's snowing. My French is terrible. Mama's living up on the fifth floor, and when I arrive she's got people with her – Frenchmen, I don't know who they were, and ladies, and some ancient Catholic priest holding a prayer-book – and the air's full of tobacco smoke, and it's bleak and uncomfortable. And suddenly I felt sorry for Mama. I felt so sorry for her I put my arms round her and pressed her head against me and couldn't let go. After that Mama kept hugging me, and crying . . .

VARYA (*on the verge of tears*). Don't, don't . . .

ANYA. She'd already sold that villa she had outside Menton. She's nothing left, nothing. Nor have I – not a kopeck. We scarcely managed it here. And Mama doesn't understand! We'll sit down to dinner in a station restaurant, and she orders the most expensive item on the menu. Then she tips all the waiters a ruble each. Charlotta's the same. And Yasha has to be fed, too – it's simply frightful. You know Mama has this footman, Yasha. We brought him with us.

VARYA. I've seen the rogue.

ANYA. So what – have we paid the interest?

VARYA. How could we?

ANYA. Oh God, oh God . . .

VARYA. In August they're going to sell the estate off.

ANYA. Oh God . . .

LOPAKHIN (*looks in at the door, and moos*). M-e-e-e . . . (*Goes out.*)

VARYA (*through her tears*). Oh, I'd like to give him such a . . . (*Raises her fist threateningly.*)

ANYA (*embraces* VARYA – *quietly*). Varya, has he proposed?

VARYA *shakes her head.*

Look, he loves you . . . Why don't you get things straight between you? What are you both waiting for?

VARYA. I'll tell you what I think – I think nothing's going to come of it. He's very busy, he hasn't got time for me – he doesn't even notice. Well, good luck to him, but I can't bear the sight of him. Everyone talks about our wedding, everyone keeps congratulating me, but in fact there's nothing there – it's all a kind of dream. (*In a different tone.*) You've got a bumble-bee brooch.

ANYA (*sadly*). Mama bought it. (*Goes into her room, and speaks cheerfully, childishly.*) And in Paris I went up in an air-balloon!

VARYA. Oh, my darling's come home! My lovely's come home again!

> DUNYASHA *is back with the coffee-pot. She makes the coffee.*
> VARYA *stands by the door to* ANYA's *room.*

Oh, my darling, I go about the house all day in a dream. If we could just get you married to some rich man, then I could be easy in my mind. I could take myself off into a retreat, then to Kiev, to Moscow, and oh, I'd walk all round the holy places . . . I'd just keep walking and walking. The glory of it!

ANYA. The birds are singing in the orchard. What time is it now?

VARYA. It must be after two. Time for you to sleep, my darling. (*Going in to* ANYA.) The glory of it!

> *Enter* YASHA *with a rug and travelling bag.*

YASHA (*crosses with delicacy*). All right to come through?

DUNYASHA. I shouldn't even recognize you, Yasha. You've changed so abroad!

YASHA. Mm . . . And who are you?

DUNYASHA. When you left I was so high . . . (*Indicates from the floor.*) Dunyasha. Fyodor Kozoyedov's daughter. You don't remember!

YASHA. Mm . . . Quite a pippin, aren't you? (*Looks round and embraces her. She screams and drops a saucer.*)

> *Exit* YASHA, *swiftly.*

VARYA (*in the doorway, displeased*). Now what's going on?

DUNYASHA (*through her tears*). I've smashed the saucer . . .

VARYA. That's good luck.

ANYA (*coming out of her room*). We should warn Mama – Petya's here.

VARYA. I gave orders not to wake him.

ANYA (*reflectively*). Six years since Father died, and only a month later that Grisha was drowned in the river. My brother . . . Seven years old, and such a pretty boy. Mama couldn't bear it. She escaped – fled without so much as a backward glance . . . (*Shivers.*) I understand her so well, if only she knew!

Pause.

And Petya Trofimov was Grisha's tutor. He may remind her . . .

Enter FIRS, *in jacket and white waistcoat.*

FIRS (*goes to the coffee-pot, preoccupied*). The mistress will be taking it in here . . . (*Puts on white gloves.*) The coffee ready? (*To* DUNYASHA, *sternly.*) What's this, girl? Where's the cream?

DUNYASHA. Oh, my Lord . . . (*Rushes out.*)

FIRS (*busies himself about the coffee-pot*). Oh, you sillybilly! (*Mutters to himself.*) Come from Paris . . . The master went to Paris once . . . by post-chaise . . . (*Laughs.*)

VARYA. What are you going on about, Firs?

FIRS. What do you want? (*Joyfully.*) My lady has come home! I waited for her! I can die happy . . . (*Weeps with joy.*)

Enter RANYEVSKAYA, GAYEV, LOPAKHIN *and* SIMEONOV-PISHCHIK *who is wearing a tight-fitting, long-waisted coat in a fine material, and wide, Oriental-looking trousers.* GAYEV, *as he comes in, makes movements with his arms and trunk as if he were playing billiards.*

RANYEVSKAYA. How did it go? Let's see . . . Yellow into the corner. Then off the cushion into the middle pocket.

GAYEV. And screw back into the corner! There was a time, my sister, when you and I slept in this very room. And now I'm fifty-one already, strange as it seems.

LOPAKHIN. Yes, the time goes by.

GAYEV. Who?

LOPAKHIN. I say the time goes by.

GAYEV. It reeks of cheap scent in here, though.

ANYA. I'm going to bed. Good night, Mama. (*Kisses her mother.*)

RANYEVSKAYA. My beloved child. (*Kisses her hands.*) Are you pleased to be home? I don't think I shall ever manage to come down to earth.

ANYA. Good night, Uncle.

GAYEV (*kisses her face and hands*). The Lord guard and keep you. How like your mother you are! (*To his sister.*) Lyuba, at her age you were just like that.

> ANYA *gives her hand to* LOPAKHIN *and* PISHCHIK, *then goes out and closes the door behind her.*

RANYEVSKAYA. She's tired out.

PISHCHIK. It's a long way to go, no doubt about it.

VARYA (*to* LOPAKHIN *and* PISHCHIK). Well, then, gentlemen. Past two o'clock. Time to be saying goodbye.

RANYEVSKAYA (*laughs*). Varya, you're just the same as ever. (*Draws her close and kisses her.*) I'll drink my coffee, then we'll all go.

> FIRS *puts a cushion under her feet.*

Thank you, my dear. I've got into the coffee habit. I drink it day and night. Thank you, my dear old friend. (*Kisses* FIRS.)

VARYA. I must see if they've brought all the things. (*Exits.*)

RANYEVSKAYA. Is this really me sitting here? (*Laughs.*) I feel like leaping into the air and waving my arms about. (*Covers her face with her hands.*) Perhaps it's all a dream. Oh, but I love my country, God knows I do, I love it tenderly. I couldn't look out of the carriage window – I did nothing but weep. (*On the verge of tears.*) However, the coffee has to be drunk. Thank you, Firs, thank you, my dear. I'm so glad to find you still alive.

FIRS. The day before yesterday.

GAYEV. His hearing's going.

LOPAKHIN. I have to leave straight away, before five o'clock. I'm off to Kharkov. Such a shame. I just wanted to get a look at you, have a few words . . . You're still as magnificent as ever.

PISHCHIK (*breathes hard*). You've grown even more lovely . . . Dressed in Paris fashions . . . I could throw caution to the winds.

LOPAKHIN. In the eyes of your sort – your brother here, for instance – I'm a boor, I'm a money-grubbing peasant, but I don't give a damn about that. The only thing I want is for you to trust me as you did before, to see your amazing, heart-breaking eyes looking at me the way they used to. Merciful God! My father was a serf, and your father and grandfather owned him. But you – yes, you were the one – you did so much for me once that I've forgotten all that, and I love you like my own flesh and blood . . . more than my own flesh and blood.

RANYEVSKAYA. I can't sit still. I'm physically incapable . . . (*Jumps up and walks about in a state of great emotion.*) I shall never survive this joy . . . Laugh at me, I'm such a fool . . . My bookcase, my own dear bookcase . . . (*Kisses the bookcase.*) My dear old table.

GAYEV. Nanna died while you were away.

RANYEVSKAYA (*sits and drinks coffee*). Yes, God rest her soul. They wrote and told me.

GAYEV. And Anastasy died. Petrushka – you remember him? With the squint? He left me. Living in town now, working for the local police inspector. (*He takes a box of fruit-drops out of his pocket and sucks one.*)

PISHCHIK. My daughter Dashenka – she sends her best regards . . .

LOPAKHIN. I want to tell you some very pleasant and cheering news. (*Glances at his watch.*) I shall be leaving very shortly, we haven't time for a proper talk . . . I'll put it in two words, then. You know, of course, that your cherry orchard is to be sold to pay your debts – the sale is fixed for the twenty-second of August. But don't you worry yourself about it, my dear – sleep easy in your bed at night – there is a way out . . . This is my plan. Now listen carefully. Your estate is only thirteen miles out

of town; the railway has now come through right next to it; and
if the cherry orchard and the land along the river are broken up
into building lots and leased out as sites for summer cottages,
then you will possess an income of – at the very least – twenty-
five thousand rubles a year.

GAYEV. I'm sorry, but it's such nonsense!

RANYEVSKAYA (*to* LOPAKHIN). I don't entirely understand
you.

LOPAKHIN. You will get from your leaseholders at the very mini-
mum ten rubles a year per acre. And if you advertise it now,
then I swear upon anything you like to name that by the autumn
you won't have a single acre left – it will all have been taken
up. In short – congratulations, you're saved. It's a marvellous
position with this deep river. The only thing, of course, is that
you need to tidy it up a bit. Remove all the old buildings, for
example – like this house, which won't have any use now – and
cut down the old cherry orchard.

RANYEVSKAYA. Cut it down? My dear, forgive me, but you don't
understand. If there is one thing of any interest at all in this
whole province – if there is even something rather remarkable –
then it's our cherry orchard.

LOPAKHIN. There's only one thing remarkable about this orchard. It's very big. You only get a full crop every other year, and
then there's nothing to do with it – no one buys it.

GAYEV. There's even a reference to this orchard in the encyclo-
paedia.

LOPAKHIN (*glances at his watch*). If we don't think of something,
if we don't come to some decision, then on the twenty-second
of August not only the cherry orchard but the whole estate
will be sold at auction. So nerve yourselves! There is no other
way out, I swear to you. None whatsoever.

FIRS. In the old days, forty, fifty years ago, they used to dry the
cherries, they used to soak them, they used to pickle them, they
used to make jam out of them, and year after year . . .

GAYEV. Do be quiet, Firs.

FIRS. And year after year they'd send off dried cherries by the cartload to Moscow and Kharkov. There was money then! And the dried cherries were soft and juicy and sweet and scented . . . They knew the recipe in those days.

RANYEVSKAYA. And what's happened to this recipe now?

FIRS. They've forgotten it. No one remembers it.

PISHCHIK (*to* RANYEVSKAYA). How was it in Paris, then? Did you eat frogs?

RANYEVSKAYA. I ate crocodiles.

PISHCHIK. Would you believe it!

LOPAKHIN. Up to now in the countryside we've had only the gentry and the peasants. But now a new class has appeared – the summer countrymen. Every town now, even the smallest, is surrounded with summer cottages. And we may assume that over the next twenty years or so our summer countryman will be fruitful and multiply exceedingly. Now he merely sits on his verandah and drinks tea, but you know it may come to pass that he'll put his couple of acres to some use, and start to cultivate them. And then this old cherry orchard of yours will become happy and rich and luxuriant . . .

GAYEV (*exasperated*). Such nonsense!

Enter VARYA *and* YASHA.

VARYA. Mama, there are two telegrams that came for you. (*Selects a key which clinks in the lock as she opens the antique bookcase.*) Here.

RANYEVSKAYA. From Paris. (*Tears up the telegrams without reading them.*) Paris is over and done with.

GAYEV. But, Lyuba, do you know how old this bookcase is? I pulled out the bottom drawer last week, and I looked, and there were some numbers burnt into the wood with a poker. This bookcase was built exactly one hundred years ago. What do you think of that? We could celebrate its centenary. It's an inanimate object, but all the same, whichever way you look at it, it's still a bookcase.

PISHCHIK (*in surprise*). A hundred years . . . Would you believe it!

GAYEV. Yes . . . Quite an achievement . . . (*Feels the bookcase.*) Dear bookcase! Most esteemed bookcase! I salute your existence, which for more than a hundred years now has been directed towards the shining ideals of goodness and of truth. For a hundred years your unspoken summons to fruitful labour has never faltered, upholding, (*on the verge of tears*) through all the generations of our family, wisdom and faith in a better future, and fostering within us ideals of goodness and of social consciousness.

Pause.

LOPAKHIN. Yes . . .

RANYEVSKAYA. You're the same as ever, Lenya.

GAYEV (*in some slight confusion*). In off into the righthand corner! Then screw back into the middle pocket!

LOPAKHIN (*glances at his watch*). Well, I must be on my way.

YASHA (*hands pills to* RANYEVSKAYA). Take your pills now, perhaps . . .

PISHCHIK. Dearest heart, you mustn't go taking medicines . . . there's neither harm nor charm in them . . . Give them here . . . Dear lady. (*Picks up the pills, tips them out on to his palm, blows on them, puts them into his mouth, and washes them down with kvass.*) There!

RANYEVSKAYA (*alarmed*). But you've gone utterly mad!

PISHCHIK. I've taken all the pills.

LOPAKHIN. There's a greedyguts!

Everyone laughs.

FIRS. When he was here at Easter he put away half a bucket of pickled cucumbers . . . (*Mutters.*)

RANYEVSKAYA. What's he going on about now?

VARYA. He's been muttering away like this for the last three years. We've got used to it.

YASHA. Old age, isn't it?

> CHARLOTTA IVANOVNA *crosses the stage, in a white dress. She is very thin and very tightly laced, with a lorgnette hanging from her belt.*

LOPAKHIN. Forgive me, I haven't had a chance to say hello to you. (*Tries to kiss her hand.*)

CHARLOTTA (*taking her hand away*). Let you kiss my hand, and next thing I know you'll be after my elbow, then my shoulder ...

LOPAKHIN. Not having any luck today, am I?

> *Everyone laughs.*

Come on, then, show us a conjuring trick!

CHARLOTTA. No, I just want to go to bed. (*Goes out.*)

LOPAKHIN. Well, we'll meet again in three weeks time. (*Kisses* RANYEVSKAYA's *hand.*) So until then. (*To* GAYEV.) Goodbye. (*Exchanges kisses with* PISHCHIK.) Goodbye. (*Gives his hand to* VARYA, *then to* FIRS *and* YASHA.) I only wish I didn't have to go. (*To* RANYEVSKAYA.) If you come to a decision about the houses, let me know, and I'll get you fifty thousand on account. Think about it seriously.

VARYA (*angrily*). Oh, go *on*!

LOPAKHIN. I'm going, I'm going. (*Exits.*)

GAYEV. A boor – the man's a boor. Oh, *pardon* ... Varya's going to marry him. He's Varya's intended.

VARYA. Uncle, please, don't start.

RANYEVSKAYA. Why, Varya, I shall be very happy. He's a good man.

PISHCHIK. A most – it has to be said – worthy man. And my Dashenka ... she also says that, well, she says various things. (*Snores, but immediately wakes up again.*) But all the same, dear lady, if you could oblige me ... with a loan of two hundred and forty rubles ... The interest on my mortgage is due tomorrow ...

VARYA (*alarmed*). No, no!

RANYEVSKAYA. I really do have nothing.

PISHCHIK. Well, it'll get itself found somehow. (*Laughs.*) I never lose hope. Here we are, I think to myself, everything's lost, I'm done for – but not at all, because lo and behold – the railway's come through my land, and . . . they've paid me. And by and by, you'll see, one day soon, something else will happen . . . There's two hundred thousand Dashenka's going to win – she's got a lucky ticket.

RANYEVSKAYA. The coffee's finished. We can go to bed.

FIRS (*brushes* GAYEV; *lecturing*). You've put the wrong trousers on again. What am I to do with you?

VARYA (*quietly*). Anya's asleep. (*Quietly opens a window.*) The sun's up already – it's not cold. Look, Mama – what marvellous trees they are! And oh, sweet heavens, the air! And the starlings are chattering!

GAYEV (*opens another window*). The orchard's all in white. You haven't forgotten, Lyuba? The way the long avenue there runs straight, straight, like a ribbon stretched taut, the way it shines on moonlit nights. You remember? You haven't forgotten?

RANYEVSKAYA (*looks out of the window at the orchard*). Oh, my childhood, my innocence! In this nursery I slept, from this room I looked out at the orchard, and happiness woke with me every morning. The orchard was just the same then, nothing has changed. (*Laughs with joy.*) All, all in white! Oh, my orchard! After dark foul autumn and cold cold winter, again you're young and filled with happiness, and not abandoned by the angels. If only the millstone could be lifted from my neck. If only I could forget my past!

GAYEV. Yes, even the orchard will be sold to meet our debts. Strange as it seems . . .

RANYEVSKAYA. Look – there's Mama, our own dead Mama, walking through the orchard . . . in a white dress! (*Laughs with joy.*) It's her.

GAYEV. Where?

VARYA. God save you, Mama.

RANYEVSKAYA. There's no one there. It just looked like it for a moment. To the right, on the turning to the summer-house – a tree bending under its blossom like the figure of a woman.

Enter TROFIMOV, *in a shabby student's uniform and spectacles.*

What an amazing orchard it is! The white masses of the blossom, the pale blue of the sky . . .

TROFIMOV. Lyubov Andreyevna!

She looks round at him.

I'm just going to pay my respects to you, and then I'll go away and leave you in peace. (*Ardently kisses her hand.*) I was told to wait until morning, but I didn't have patience enough.

RANYEVSKAYA *gazes at him in perplexity.*

VARYA (*on the verge of tears*). It's Petya.

TROFIMOV. Trofimov. Petya Trofimov. I used to be Grisha's tutor . . . Have I really changed so much?

RANYEVSKAYA *embraces him and weeps quietly.*

GAYEV (*embarrassed*). Come on, Lyuba. Come on, now.

VARYA (*weeps*). Petya, I did tell you to wait until tomorrow.

RANYEVSKAYA. My Grisha . . . my boy . . . Grisha . . . my son . . .

VARYA. What can we do, Mama? It was God's will.

TROFIMOV (*softly, on the verge of tears*). There now . . . There, now . . .

RANYEVSKAYA (*weeps quietly*). My boy died, my little boy was drowned . . . Why? Why, my friend? (*More quietly.*) Anya's asleep in there, and here am I talking at the top of my voice . . . making a noise . . . What's this, Petya? Why have you lost your looks? Why have you aged so?

TROFIMOV. You know what some old woman on a train the other day called me? – 'That mangy-looking gentleman.'

RANYEVSKAYA. You were still only a boy before, just a nice

young student. Now you've got glasses, your hair's gone thin. You're surely not still a student? (*Goes to the door.*)

TROFIMOV. I should think I'm going to be a perpetual student. The Wandering Student, like the Wandering Jew.

RANYEVSKAYA (*kisses her brother, then* VARYA). Well, off to bed, then . . . You've aged, too, Leonid.

PISHCHIK (*follows her*). So, bedtime . . . Oh, my gout. I'll stay the night here, I think. (*To* RANYEVSKAYA.) And in the morning, dearest heart, if you would . . . two hundred and forty rubles . . .

GAYEV. Never gives up, does he?

PISHCHIK. Two hundred and forty rubles . . . I have to pay the interest on my mortgage.

RANYEVSKAYA. I have no money, my sweet.

PISHCHIK. I'll give it back, my dear. It's the most piffling sum.

RANYEVSKAYA. Well, all right. Leonid will give it to you. You give it to him, Leonid.

GAYEV. If it's up to me, he can whistle for it.

RANYEVSKAYA. What can we do? Just give it to him . . . He needs it . . . He'll give it back.

Exeunt RANYEVSKAYA, TROFIMOV, PISHCHIK *and* FIRS.

GAYEV, VARYA *and* YASHA *remain.*

GAYEV. My sister still hasn't got out of the habit of flinging her money around. (*To* YASHA.) Do go away, my dear good chap – you smell of chickens.

YASHA (*grinning*). And you're just the same as you always were.

GAYEV. Who? (*To* VARYA.) What does he say?

VARYA (*to* YASHA). Your mother's come from the village. She's been sitting in the servants' hall since yesterday waiting to see you.

YASHA. Well, good luck to her, then.

VARYA. Shameless, aren't you?

YASHA. What's the point. She could just as well have come tomorrow. (*Goes out.*)

VARYA. Mama's exactly the same as she was. She hasn't changed at all. If it was up to her she'd have given everything away.

GAYEV. Yes . . .

Pause.

If for some disease a great many different remedies are proposed, then it means that the disease is incurable. I think, I cudgel my brains – I have many remedies, a great many – and what that means when you get down to it is that I haven't a solitary one. It would be a good thing if we got an inheritance from someone. It would be a good thing if we married Anya to some very rich man. It would be a good thing if we went to Yaroslavl and tried our luck with that aunt of ours, the countess. She's very rich indeed, you know.

VARYA (*weeps*). If only God would help.

GAYEV. Don't howl. Aunt is very rich, but she doesn't like us. In the first place, my sister married an ordinary lawyer instead of a gentleman with property . . .

ANYA *appears in the doorway*.

She married a commoner, and the way she's behaved – well, you couldn't say it was very virtuously. She's good, she's kind, she's a splendid woman, I love her dearly, but however many extenuating circumstances you think up, the fact has to be faced: she is depraved. You can sense it in her slightest movement.

VARYA (*in a whisper*). Anya is standing in the doorway.

GAYEV. Who?

Pause.

Funny – I've got something in my right eye. I can't see properly. And on Thursday, when I was at the district court . . .

Enter ANYA.

VARYA. Why aren't you asleep, Anya?

ANYA. I can't get to sleep.

GAYEV. My pet. (*Kisses* ANYA's *face and hands*.) My child . . . (On the verge of tears.) You're not my niece – you're my angel. You're everything to me. Believe me. Trust me.

ANYA. I trust you, uncle. Everyone loves you, everyone looks up to you . . . but, dear Uncle, you must be quiet, only be quiet. What were you saying just then about my mother – about your own sister? Why did you say that?

GAYEV. Yes, yes . . . (*Covers his face with her hand*.) Really, that was terrible! God forgive me! And today I made a speech to the bookcase . . . so stupid! And only when I'd finished did I realize how stupid it was.

VARYA. It's true, Uncle dear, you must keep quiet. Just be quiet, that's all.

ANYA. If you're quiet, you'll be calmer in yourself, too.

GAYEV. I am silent. (*Kisses their hands*.) Not a word. Just one thing on a matter of business. On Thursday I was at the district court, and, well, a few of us there got talking about this and that, one thing and another, and it seems it would be possible to arrange a loan against my note of hand to pay the bank interest.

VARYA. If only the Lord would help!

GAYEV. On Tuesday I'll go and have another talk about it. (*To* VARYA.) Don't howl. (*To* ANYA.) Your mother will have a word with Lopakhin. He obviously won't refuse her. And you – as soon as you've got your breath back you'll go to Yaroslavl to see the countess, your great aunt. So we'll be operating from three sides at once – and the job's as good as done. We shall pay the interest, of that I'm convinced. (*Puts a fruit drop in his mouth*.) I swear, upon my honour, upon whatever you like, that the estate will not be sold! (*Excitedly*.) By my hope of happiness I swear it! Here's my hand on it – call me a low, dishonourable fellow if I let it go to auction! By my whole being I swear to you!

ANYA (*her calm mood has returned to her: she is happy*). What a good man you are, Uncle, what a good and clever man! (*Embraces him.*) Now I'm calm! Quite calm! I'm happy!

Enter FIRS.

FIRS (*to* GAYEV, *reproachfully*). What? Have you no fear before God? When are you going to bed?

GAYEV. Right now, right now. You go off. Don't worry about me, I'll undress myself. Well, night night, then, children. Details tomorrow, but now to bed. (*Kisses* ANYA *and* VARYA.) I am a man of the eighties. Not a period they speak well of these days, but I can tell you that I have suffered not a little in this life for my convictions. It's no accident that your ordinary peasant loves me. You have to know your peasant! You have to know how to . . .

ANYA. Uncle, you're off again!

VARYA. Dear uncle, just be quiet.

FIRS (*angrily*). Leonid Andreyich!

GAYEV. I'm coming, I'm coming . . . Off to bed, then. Cushion, cushion, and into the middle pocket! Clean as a whistle . . . (*Goes out, with* FIRS *trotting behind him.*)

ANYA. Now I'm calm. I don't want to go to Yaroslavl – I don't like our great aunt. But all the same I'm calm. Thanks to Uncle. (*Sits down.*)

VARYA. We must get some sleep. I'm off. One rather annoying thing happened while you were away, though. You know what used to be the servants' quarters? Well, of course, it's only the elderly servants who live there now: Yefimushka, Polya, Yevstigney, oh, yes, and Karp. Well, they began to let various riff-raff in to spend the night. I said nothing about it. Only then I hear they've been spreading a rumour to the effect that I've had them fed on nothing but dried peas. Out of meanness, do you see . . . And all this is Yevstigney's doing . . . Right, I think to myself. If that's the way you want it, then just you wait. So I send for Yevstigney . . . (*Yawns.*) He comes in . . .

What's all this, then, Yevstigney? I say to him . . . You're such a fool . . . (*Looks at* ANYA.) Anyechka . . . !

Pause.

Asleep . . . ! (*Takes* ANYA *by the arm.*) Off we go to bed, then . . . Off we go . . . ! (*Leads her.*) My poor precious has fallen fast asleep! Off we go . . .

A long way away, beyond the orchard, a SHEPHERD *plays on a reed pipe.*

TROFIMOV *crosses the stage, and stops at the sight of* VARYA *and* ANYA.

VARYA. Sh . . . She's asleep . . . asleep . . . Off we go, my own sweet precious.

ANYA (*quietly, half asleep*). So tired . . . I can still hear the harness bells . . . Uncle . . . dear Uncle . . . Mama and Uncle, too . . .

VARYA. Off we go, my own sweet love. Off we go . . .

They go into ANYA's *room.*

TROFIMOV (*moved*). My sunshine! My springtime!

CURTAIN

Act Two

The open fields. A wayside shrine – old, crooked, and long neglected. Beside it – a well, large slabs which were evidently once tombstones, and an old bench. A path can be seen leading to the Gayev estate. At one side rise the dark shapes of poplars; this is where the cherry orchard begins.

In the distance is a row of telegraph poles, and a long way away on the horizon a large town can just be made out, visible only in very fine, clear weather. The sun is just about to set.

CHARLOTTA, YASHA and DUNYASHA are sitting on the bench; YEPIKHODOV is standing beside it, playing the guitar. They are all in a reflective mood.

CHARLOTTA is wearing an old peaked cap. She has taken a gun off her shoulder and is adjusting the buckle on the sling.

CHARLOTTA (*meditatively*). I haven't got proper papers – I don't know how old I am. So I always think of myself as being young. When I was a little girl Mama and my father used to go round all the fairs giving shows. Very good shows they were, too. And I'd turn somersaults and do all kinds of little tricks. And when Papa and Mama died, some German lady took me in and began to give me an education. So, all right, I grew up, and then I went to be a governess. But where I come from and who I am, I don't know. Who my parents were – whether they were even married or not – I don't know. (*Gets a cucumber out of her pocket and eats it.*) I don't know anything.

Pause.

I so long to talk to someone, but there's no one to talk to. I haven't got anyone.

YEPIKHODOV (*plays the guitar and sings*).
What should I care for life's clamour,
What for my friend or my foe . . .

How very agreeable it is to pluck at the strings of a mandoline!

DUNYASHA. That's not a mandoline – that's a guitar. (*Powders herself in a pocket mirror.*)

YEPIKHODOV. For the madman who's in love it's a mandoline. (*Sings.*)

. . . Had I a passion requited
Warming my heart with its glow?

YASHA *joins in.*

CHARLOTTA. Horrible way these people sing! Faugh! Like jackals howling!

DUNYASHA (*to* YASHA). All the same, how lovely to spend some time abroad.

YASHA. Yes, of course. I couldn't agree more. (*Yawns, and then lights a cigar.*)

YEPIKHODOV. Oh, absolutely. Everything abroad's been in full constitution for years.

YASHA. Obviously.

YEPIKHODOV. Here am I – I mean, I'm a grown man – I read – I read all sorts of important books – but what I can't make out is any I mean kind of movement of opinion when it comes to what I personally want in life. Put it this way – do I want to go on living, or do I want to shoot myself? I mean, I always carry a revolver on me, look. (*Shows the revolver.*)

CHARLOTTA. Done it. I'm off. (*Slings the gun on her shoulder.*) Yepikhodov, you're a genius. A terrifying genius. All the women ought to be mad about you. Brrr! (*Starts to go.*) These great brains – they're all such fools. I've no one to talk to. Alone, always alone, I haven't got anyone. And who I am and why I am remains a mystery . . . (*Goes unhurriedly off.*)

YEPIKHODOV. I mean, leaving everything else aside, I mean just taking my own case, and I'm not going to mince my words, but, really, fate has treated me quite relentlessly. I've been tossed around like a rowing-boat in a high sea. All right, let's say I'm talking nonsense. In that case, why, just to take one example, why, when I woke up this morning, why did I find, sitting there on my chest, this enormous spider? Like this. (*Demonstrates with both hands.*) All right, take another example. I pour myself some kvass, to have a drink, and there in the glass is something really profoundly horrible. I mean, a cockroach, for example.

Pause.

Have you read Buckle? The History of Civilization?

Pause

(*To* DUNYASHA.) If I might trouble you, I should appreciate the chance of a word or two.

DUNYASHA. Go on, then.

YEPIKHODOV. I should have been hopeful of having it in private. (*Sighs.*)

DUNYASHA (*embarrassed*). All right – only first fetch me my cloak. You'll find it by the cupboard. It's rather damp here.

YEPIKHODOV. Now I know what to do with my revolver . . . (*Takes his guitar and goes off playing it.*)

YASHA. Poor old Disasters! Between you and me, that man is a fool. (*Yawns.*)

DUNYASHA. Just so long as he doesn't go and shoot himself.

Pause.

I've got so nervy these days – I worry all the time. They took me into service when I was a little girl still. I've got out of the way of ordinary people's life now. Look at my hands – white as white, like a lady's. I've turned into someone all refined, some-one terribly delicate and ladylike – I'm frightened of every-thing. It's dreadful being like this. And Yasha, if you deceive me, well, I don't know what would become of my nerves.

YASHA (*kisses her*). Real country pippin, aren't you? Of course, every girl's got to remember who she is. If there's one thing I hate more than anything else, it's a girl who doesn't know how to behave herself.

DUNYASHA. I'm absolutely passionately in love with you. Because you're an educated man – you can talk about anything.

> *Pause.*

YASHA (*yawns*). Right . . . What I think is, if a girl's in love with someone then she's got no morals.

> *Pause.*

Nice having a cigar in the open air . . . (*Listens.*) Someone coming . . . It's *them.*

> DUNYASHA *impetuously embraces him.*

Go home as if you'd been down to the river for a swim – here, along this path. Otherwise you'll run into them and they'll think I've been seeing you. I'm not having that.

DUNYASHA (*coughs quietly*). Your cigar's given me a headache . . . (*Goes off.*)

> YASHA *remains, sitting beside the shrine.*

> *Enter* RANYEVSKAYA, GAYEV, *and* LOPAKHIN.

LOPAKHIN. It has to be settled once and for all – time won't wait. Look, it's a simple enough question. Do you agree to lease out the land for summer cottages or not? Answer me one word: yes or no? Just one word!

RANYEVSKAYA. Who's smoking some foul cigar? (*Sits.*)

GAYEV. It's very convenient now they've built the railway. (*Sits.*) We popped into town and had some lunch . . . Yellow into the middle pocket! I should have gone indoors first and had a quick game.

RANYEVSKAYA. You've still got time.

LOPAKHIN. Just one word! (*Pleading.*) Give me an answer!

GAYEV (*yawns*). Who?

RANYEVSKAYA (*looks into her purse*). There was a lot of money in here yesterday, and today there's hardly any. My poor Varya feeds everyone on milk soup to economize – she gives the old men in the kitchen nothing but dried peas, while I somehow just go on mindlessly spending . . . (*Drops the purse and scatters gold coins.*) And now it's gone everywhere . . . (*She is annoyed.*)

YASHA. Leave it to me – I'll do it. (*Picks up the coins.*)

RANYEVSKAYA. Would you, Yasha? And why did I go into town for lunch? That horrible restaurant of yours with the music playing, and the tablecloths smelling of soap . . . Why do you drink so much, Lenya? Why do you eat so much? Why do you talk so much? In the restaurant today you kept talking again – and it was all so rambling. The seventies, the Decadent movement. And who were you saying it all to? Fancy telling the waiters about the Decadents!

LOPAKHIN. Yes.

GAYEV (*waves his hand*). I'm incorrigible, that's obvious. (*To* YASHA, *irritated.*) What is it? You're perpetually dangling in front of my eyes.

YASHA (*laughs*). I can't hear your voice without wanting to laugh.

GAYEV (*to his sister*). Either he goes, or I do.

RANYEVSKAYA. Off you go, Yasha.

YASHA (*gives* RANYEVSKAYA *her purse*). Certainly. (*Scarcely restrains himself from laughing.*) This instant. (*Goes.*)

LOPAKHIN. Your estate is going to be bought by Deriganov. He's a very wealthy man. I gather he's coming to the sale in person.

RANYEVSKAYA. Where did you hear that?

LOPAKHIN. It's what they're saying in town.

GAYEV. Our aunt in Yaroslavl has promised to send something, but when and how much – that we don't know.

LOPAKHIN. What would it be? A hundred thousand? Two hundred thousand?

RANYEVSKAYA. Ten or fifteen thousand, and lucky if we get even that.

LOPAKHIN. Forgive me for saying this, but such frivolous people as you, such strange unbusinesslike people, I have never come across. You are told in plain language that your estate is being sold, and you simply do not understand.

RANYEVSKAYA. What can we possibly do? Tell us.

LOPAKHIN. I tell you every day. Every day I tell you exactly the same thing. The cherry orchard and the land along the river must be leased out for summer cottages – and it must be done now, as soon as possible – the sale is upon us! Get it into your heads! Just once make up your minds to have the houses and you will get money – as much money as you like – and you will be saved.

RANYEVSKAYA. Summer cottages – summer people – forgive me, but it's so squalid.

GAYEV. I agree entirely.

LOPAKHIN. I don't know whether to scream, or to burst into tears, or to fall down in a faint. I can't go on! You reduce me to despair! (*To* GAYEV.) You're an old woman!

GAYEV. Who?

LOPAKHIN. An old woman. You! (*Starts to go.*)

RANYEVSKAYA (*frightened*). No, don't go. Stay with us, my dear. I beg you. Perhaps we'll think of something.

LOPAKHIN. What is there to think of?

RANYEVSKAYA. Don't go, I implore you. It's more fun with you here, at any rate . . .

Pause.

I keep waiting for something to happen – as if the house were going to come down about our ears.

GAYEV (*deep in thought*). Red, cushion, and into the corner . . . Cushion, red, and into the corner . . .

RANYEVSKAYA. We have sinned, and sinned greatly . . .

LOPAKHIN. What are your sins, then?

GAYEV (*puts a fruit drop in his mouth*). They say I've wasted all my substance in fruit drops ... (*Laughs.*)

RANYEVSKAYA. Oh, my sins ... Always I've thrown money about like a lunatic, and I married a man who made nothing of his life but debts. My husband died of champagne – he was a terrible drinker – and my misfortune then was to fall in love with someone else. I gave myself to him, and it was just at that time – and this was my first punishment, it was like a club coming down on my head – my little boy ... in the river here ... my little boy was drowned, and I went away, went abroad, went utterly away, went meaning never to return, never to see this river again ... I shut my eyes, ran blindly – and *he* after me ... pitilessly, brutally. I bought a villa outside Menton, because *he* fell sick there, and for three years I knew no rest, neither by day nor by night. For three years he was an invalid – he drained my strength – my spirit broke. And last year, when the villa was sold to pay my debts, I went to Paris, and there he robbed me openly, he threw me aside, he took up with another woman. I tried to poison myself ... So stupid, so shameful ... And suddenly I yearned for Russia, for my homeland, for my daughter ... (*Wipes her tears.*) Lord, Lord have mercy! Forgive me my sins! Don't punish me any more! (*Takes a telegram out of her pocket.*) I got this today from Paris ... He begs my forgiveness, implores me to return ... (*Tears the telegram up.*) There's a sound of music somewhere. (*Listens.*)

GAYEV. That's our famous Jewish orchestra. Do you remember? Four fiddles, flute, and double bass.

RANYEVSKAYA. It still exists? We ought to get them here somehow – we ought to arrange an evening.

LOPAKHIN (*listens*). I can't hear anything ...
(*Sings quietly.*)
> *Money talks, so here's poor Russkies*
> *Getting Frenchified by Germans.*

(*Laughs.*) Very good play I saw last night. Very funny.

RANYEVSKAYA. There's nothing funny in the world. People shouldn't watch plays. They should look at their own selves a little more often. What grey lives they all lead. How much they say that should never be said at all.

LOPAKHIN. True. We live like complete fools, it has to be admitted.

Pause.

My father was a peasant. He was an idiot, he knew nothing, he taught me nothing, all he did was to take his stick to me when he was drunk. And when you get down to it, I'm just the same sort of stupid oaf myself. I've never learnt anything. I write such a foul hand I'm ashamed for people to see it. I'm a pig.

RANYEVSKAYA. What you need, my friend, is to get married.

LOPAKHIN. Yes . . . That's true.

RANYEVSKAYA. To Varya, why not? Our own Varya. She's a good girl.

LOPAKHIN. Yes.

RANYEVSKAYA. She came to me from simple people – she works the whole day long. But the main thing is, she loves you. Yes, and you've liked her for a long time now.

LOPAKHIN. Fair enough. I've nothing against it. She's a good girl.

Pause.

GAYEV. I've been offered a job in a bank. Six thousand a year. Have you heard about that?

RANYEVSKAYA. The idea! You just stay as you are.

Enter FIRS. *He has brought an overcoat.*

FIRS (*to* GAYEV). Now will you put it on, sir, if you please, or you'll be getting damp.

GAYEV (*puts on the coat*). Firs, my friend, you're a bore.

FIRS. No call for that, now. You went off this morning without a word. (*Examines him.*)

RANYEVSKAYA. You've aged, Firs, haven't you?

FIRS. What do you want?

LOPAKHIN. She says you've aged a lot!

FIRS. I've lived a long life. They were marrying me off before your Papa even arrived in the world. (*Laughs.*) And when the Freedom came, in sixty-one, I was already head valet. I didn't agree to have the Freedom – I stayed with the masters . . .

Pause.

And I remember, everyone was glad. But what they were glad about they didn't know themselves.

LOPAKHIN. Lovely it was before. At least they flogged you.

FIRS (*not having heard right*). Oh, my word, they were. The peasants belonged to the masters, and the masters to the peasants. Now it's all chippety-choppety – you can't make any sense of it.

GAYEV. Do be quiet for a moment, Firs. Tomorrow I have to go into town. I've been promised an introduction to a general who might put up something against my note of hand.

LOPAKHIN. Nothing's going to come of it, whatever you do. And you're not going to pay that interest, don't worry.

RANYEVSKAYA. He's living in a dream. There's no general.

Enter TROFIMOV, ANYA *and* VARYA.

GAYEV. Some more of us coming.

ANYA. It's Mama.

RANYEVSKAYA (*tenderly*). Here . . . here . . . my own darlings . . . (*Embracing* ANYA *and* VARYA.) If only you knew how much I love you both! Sit next to me – here . . .

They all settle themselves down.

LOPAKHIN. Our Wandering Student always seems to be wandering with the young ladies.

TROFIMOV. Mind your own business.

LOPAKHIN. He'll be fifty before he knows where he is, and still a student.

TROFIMOV. Why don't you leave off your stupid jokes?

LOPAKHIN. Not losing your temper, are you, O weird one?

TROFIMOV. Don't keep badgering me.

LOPAKHIN (*laughs*). All right, then, my dear sir. What do you make of me?

TROFIMOV. I'll tell you what I make of you, sir. You're a wealthy man – you'll soon be a millionaire. And just as there must be predatory animals to maintain nature's metabolism by devouring whatever crosses their path, so there must also be you.

They all laugh.

VARYA. Petya, I think it would be better if you told us about the planets.

RANYEVSKAYA. No, let's go on with the conversation we were having yesterday.

TROFIMOV. What was that about?

GAYEV. Pride.

TROFIMOV. We talked for a long time yesterday, but we never arrived at any conclusions. Human pride, in the sense you're using it, has some kind of mystical significance. And you may even be right, in your own fashion. But if we're going to talk about it in a down-to-earth way, without any fancy trimmings, then what sort of pride can there be – does the expression have any sense at all – if man is physiologically ill-constructed, if in the vast majority of cases he is crude and stupid and profoundly unhappy? We have to stop admiring ourselves. We have simply to work.

GAYEV. It makes no difference – you still die.

TROFIMOV. Who knows? And what does it mean – you die? Perhaps man has a hundred senses, and at death it's only the five we know of that perish, while the other ninety-five go on living.

RANYEVSKAYA. What a clever man you are, Petya!

LOPAKHIN (*ironically*). Oh, staggeringly.

TROFIMOV. Mankind is advancing, perfecting its powers. All the things that are beyond its reach now will one day be brought close and made plain. All we have to do is to work, to bend all our strength to help those who are seeking the truth. Here in Russia very few as yet are working. Most members of the intelligentsia, so far as I know it, are seeking nothing, neither the truth nor anything else. They're doing nothing – they're still incapable of hard work. They call themselves the intelligentsia, but they treat servants like children, and peasants like animals. They don't know how to study. They never do any serious reading. They understand next to nothing about art; science they merely talk about. They're all terribly serious people with terribly stern expressions on their faces. They all talk about nothing but terribly important questions. They all philosophize away. And right in front of their eyes the whole time there are workers living on filthy food and sleeping without pillows to their heads, thirty and forty to a room – and everywhere bugs, damp, stench, and moral squalor. And all the fine conversations we have are plainly just to distract attention from it all. Our own attention, and other people's, too. Show me – where are the crèches that everyone's always going on about – where are the reading-rooms? They're only in novels – they don't exist in reality. There's just filth and banality and barbarism. I have little love for all those serious faces; I fear those serious conversations. Better to be silent.

LOPAKHIN. Listen, I get up before five every morning, I work all the hours God gave, I'm constantly handling money – my own and other people's – and I can't help seeing what my fellow men are like. You've only got to start trying to do something to discover how few honest, decent people there are in the world. Sometimes, when I can't sleep, I think to myself: 'Lord, you gave us immense forests, boundless plains, broad horizons – living in it all we ought properly to be giants.'

RANYEVSKAYA. A lot of use giants would be. They're all right in fairy-tales. Anywhere else they're frightening.

YEPIKHODOV *crosses upstage, playing the guitar.*

(*Pensively.*) There goes Yepikhodov . . .

ANYA (*likewise*). There goes Yepikhodov . . .

GAYEV. The sun has set, ladies and gentlemen.

TROFIMOV. Yes.

GAYEV (*softly, as if declaiming*). O nature, wondrous nature! You shine with an everlasting radiance, beautiful and indifferent; you that we call Mother unite within yourself existence and death; you give life and you destroy it . . .

VARYA (*imploringly*). Uncle!

ANYA. You're doing it again!

TROFIMOV. You'd be better off potting yellow.

GAYEV. I am silent, I am silent.

They all sit lost in thought. Silence. All that can be heard is FIRS *muttering quietly. Suddenly there is a distant sound, as if from the sky: the sound of a breaking string – dying away, sad.*

RANYEVSKAYA. What was that?

LOPAKHIN. I don't know. Somewhere a long way off, in the mines, a winding cable has parted. But a long, long way off.

GAYEV. Perhaps a bird of some sort . . . something like a heron.

TROFIMOV. Or some kind of owl.

RANYEVSKAYA (*shivers*). Horrible, I don't know why.

Pause.

FIRS. It was the same before the troubles. The owl screeched, and the samovar moaned without stop.

GAYEV. Before what troubles?

FIRS. Before the Freedom.

Pause.

RANYEVSKAYA. Listen, my friends, we must be going. The night is drawing on. (*To* ANYA.) There are tears in your eyes. What is it, child? (*Embraces her.*)

ANYA. Nothing. Just tears. It doesn't matter.

TROFIMOV. There's someone coming.

A PASSER-BY *appears. He is wearing an overcoat and a stolen white peaked cap; he is slightly drunk.*

PASSER-BY. Begging your pardon – can I get through this way to the station?

GAYEV. Yes. Along this path.

PASSER-BY. Most profoundly grateful. (*Coughs.*) Wonderful weather . . . (*Declaims.*)

> My friend, my brother, weary, suffering, sad,
> Though falsehood rule and evil triumph,
> Take courage yet and let your soul be glad . . .

Pause.

> Go to the Volga. Hear again
> The song it sings, the song of groans –
> The litany of hauling men,
> Groaned from weary hearts and bones.
> Volga! All spring's melted snows,
> And still you cannot flood your plain
> As wide as this land overflows
> With all its people's sea of pain . . .

(*To* VARYA) Mademoiselle, spare a few kopeks for a starving Russian.

VARYA is frightened, and cries out.

LOPAKHIN (*angrily*). Now that's enough! There are limits!

RANYEVSKAYA (*hurriedly*). Wait . . . here you are . . . (*Looks in her purse.*) I've no silver . . . Never mind, here – ten rubles . . . (*Gives him a gold coin.*)

PASSER-BY. Most profoundly grateful. (*Goes off.*)

Laughter.

VARYA (*frightened*). I'm going in . . . Oh, Mama – at home there's nothing for the servants to eat, and you gave him ten rubles.

RANYEVSKAYA. What's to be done with me? – I'm so silly! When we get home I'll give you everything I've got. (*To* LOPAKHIN.) You'll lend me some more, won't you?

LOPAKHIN. Your humble servant.

RANYEVSKAYA. Ladies and gentlemen, it's time we were going. Oh, and Varya, while we were sitting here we quite made a match for you. So congratulations.

VARYA (*on the verge of tears*). Don't joke about it, Mama.

LOPAKHIN. Get thee to a nunnery, Ophelia-Ophoolia.

GAYEV. My hands are shaking – I've been missing my billiards.

LOPAKHIN. Nymph, in thy orisons be all my sins dismembered!

RANYEVSKAYA. Off we go, then. It's nearly time for supper.

VARYA. He gave me such a fright. My heart's simply pounding.

LOPAKHIN. Let me remind you, ladies and gentlemen: the cherry orchard will be coming up for sale on the twenty-second of August. Think about it! Think!

They all go out except TROFIMOV *and* ANYA.

ANYA (*laughing*). We ought to thank that tramp for frightening Varya. Now we're alone.

TROFIMOV. She's afraid you and I are suddenly going to fall in love with each other. She doesn't let us out of her sight for days at a time. What she can't get into her narrow mind is that we're above such things as love. Our whole aim – the whole sense of our life – is to avoid the petty illusions that stop us being free and happy. On, on, on! We are going to that bright star that blazes from afar there, and no one can hold us back! On, on, on! In step together, friends!

ANYA (*clasping her hands*). How beautifully you talk!

Pause.

It's wonderful here today.

TROFIMOV. Yes, amazing weather.

ANYA. What have you done to me, Petya? Why don't I love the cherry orchard like I used to? I loved it so tenderly. I thought there was nowhere finer on earth.

TROFIMOV. All Russia is our orchard. The earth is broad and beautiful. There are many marvellous places.

Pause.

Think for a moment, Anya: your grandfather, your great-grandfather – all your forebears – they were the masters of serfs. They owned living souls. Can't you see human faces, looking out at you from behind every tree-trunk in the orchard – from every leaf and every cherry? Can't you hear their voices? The possession of living souls – it's changed something deep in all of you, hasn't it. So that your mother and you and your uncle don't even notice you're living on credit, at the expense of others – at the expense of people you don't allow past the front hall . . . We're two hundred years behind the times at least. We still have nothing – no properly defined attitude to the past. We just philosophize away, and complain about our boredom or drink vodka. But it's only too clear that to start living in the present we have to redeem our past – we have to break with it. And it can be redeemed only by suffering, only by the most unheard-of, unceasing labour. You must understand that, Anya.

ANYA. The house we live in hasn't been ours for a long time now. I'm going to leave, I give you my word.

TROFIMOV. Throw the keys down the well, and go. Be free as the wind.

ANYA (*in delight*). You put it so beautifully!

TROFIMOV. Have faith in me, Anya! Have faith in me! I'm not thirty yet – I'm young – I'm still a student – but I've borne so much already! Every winter I'm hungry, sick and fearful, as poor as a beggar. And the places I've been to! The places where fate has driven me! And all the time, at every minute of the day and night, my soul has been filled with premonitions I can't explain or describe. I have a premonition of happiness, Anya. I can just see it now . . .

ANYA (*pensively*). The moon is rising.

There is the sound of YEPIKHODOV *still playing the same mournful song on his guitar. The moon rises. Somewhere over by the poplar trees* VARYA *is looking for* ANYA.

VARYA (*calling off*). Anya! Where are you?
TROFIMOV. Yes, the moon is rising.

Pause.

Here it is – happiness. Here it comes. Closer and closer. I can hear its footsteps already. And if we don't see it, if we never know its face, then what does it matter? Others will!

VARYA (*off*). Anya! Where are you?
TROFIMOV. There's that Varya again! (*Angrily.*) It's outrageous!
ANYA. Come on – let's go down to the river. It's nice there.
TROFIMOV. Come on, then.

They start to go.

VARYA (*off*). Anya! Anya!

CURTAIN

Act Three

The drawing-room, with an archway leading through into the ball-room. The chandelier is lit.

From an ante-room comes the sound of the Jewish orchestra mentioned in Act Two. Company has been invited for the evening. In the ballroom they are dancing the 'grand-rond'.

SIMEONOV-PISHCHIK (*off*). *Promenade à une paire!*

> *The* COUPLES *emerge into the drawing-room – first* PISHCHIK *and* CHARLOTTA IVANOVNA, *second* TROFIMOV *and* RANYEVSKAYA, *third* ANYA *and the* POSTMASTER, *fourth* VARYA *and the* STATIONMASTER, *and so on.* VARYA *is quietly weeping, and wiping her eyes as she dances. In the last couple is* DUNYASHA. *They go round the room.*

PISHCHIK. *Grand-rond balancez . . .! Les cavaliers à genoux et remerciez vos dames!*

> FIRS, *wearing a tailcoat, brings the seltzer water on a tray.* PISHCHIK *and* TROFIMOV *come into the drawing-room.*

PISHCHIK. Blood-pressure – that's my trouble. I've had two strokes already, and I don't find dancing easy. But you know what they say – if you run with the pack you must wag your tail. I'm as strong as a horse. My late father, who was something of a humourist, God rest his soul, used to say the venerable tribe of Simeonov-Pishchik was descended from the horse that Caligula made consul . . . (*Sits down.*) But the snag is – no money! What do people say? – A hungry dog believes only in meat . . . (*Snores and immediately wakes up again.*) Same with me – can't think about anything but money.

TROFIMOV. It's true – there is something rather horse-like about you.

PISHCHIK. Well, that's all right . . . a horse is a good beast . . . a horse can be sold.

There is the sound of billiards being played in the next room. VARYA *appears in the archway to the ballroom.*

TROFIMOV (*teasing*). Madame Lopakhina! Madame Lopakhina!

VARYA (*angrily*). And who's this? The mangy-looking gentleman.

TROFIMOV. Yes, that's what I am – a mangy-looking gentleman. And proud of it!

VARYA (*reflecting bitterly*). Here we are, we've hired musicians – but what are we going to pay them with? (*Goes out.*)

TROFIMOV (*to* PISHCHIK). If all the energy you've expended during your life in the quest for money had gone on something else, you could have turned the world upside down by now.

PISHCHIK. Nietzsche – the philosopher – very great philosopher, very famous one – man of enormous intelligence – he claims in his books that it's all right to forge banknotes.

TROFIMOV. You've read Nietzsche, have you?

PISHCHIK. Well . . . my daughter Dashenka was telling me about him. Though with the position I'm in now, even if I started forging banknotes . . . I've got to pay three hundred and ten rubles the day after tomorrow . . . I've got hold of a hundred and thirty . . . (*Feels his pockets in alarm.*) The money's gone! I've lost the money! (*On the verge of tears.*). Where's the money? (*Joyfully.*) Here it is, in the lining . . . I'd quite come out in a sweat.

Enter RANYEVSKAYA *and* CHARLOTTA IVANOVNA.

RANYEVSKAYA (*hums a Caucasian dance, the lezghinka*). Why is Leonid taking so long? What can he be doing in town? (*To* DUNYASHA.) Dunyasha, ask the musicians if they'd like some tea.

TROFIMOV. The sale probably never took place.

RANYEVSKAYA. It wasn't the moment to have the band, it wasn't the moment to get up a ball. Well, who cares? (*Sits down and hums quietly.*)

CHARLOTTA (*offers* PISHCHIK *a pack of cards*). Think of a card. Any card you like.

PISHCHIK. I've thought of one.

CHARLOTTA. Now shuffle the pack. Good. Give it to me, then, my dear monsieur Pishchik. *Ein, zwei, drei!* Now have a look and you'll find it in your side pocket.

PISHCHIK (*gets a card out of his side pocket*). The eight of spades – that's absolutely right! (*Amazed.*) Well, would you believe it!

CHARLOTTA (*to* TROFIMOV, *holding the pack in the palm of her hand*). The top card – quick – what is it?

TROFIMOV. I don't know . . . oh . . . the queen of spades.

CHARLOTTA. Right! (*To* PISHCHIK.) Well? The top card?

PISHCHIK. The ace of hearts.

CHARLOTTA. Right! (*Claps her hands, and the pack disappears.*) Marvellous weather we're having!

A mysterious female voice answers, apparently from under the floor.

VOICE. Oh, yes, wonderful weather!

CHARLOTTA. You are my heart's ideal!

VOICE. Yes, I've taken rather a fancy to you.

STATIONMASTER (*applauds*). Madame the ventriloquist! Bravo!

PISHCHIK (*amazed*). Would you believe it! Enchanting woman! I've absolutely fallen in love with you.

CHARLOTTA. In love? (*Shrugs her shoulders.*) Are you really capable of love? *Guter Mensch, aber schlechter Musikant.*

TROFIMOV (*claps* PISHCHIK *on the shoulder*). You're so much like a horse, you see . . .

CHARLOTTA. Your attention please. One more trick. (*Takes a travelling rug off one of the chairs.*) I have here a very fine rug, a very fine rug for sale. (*Shakes it.*) Who'll buy this very fine rug?

PISHCHIK (*amazed*). Would you believe it!

CHARLOTTA. *Ein, zwei, drei!* (*She has lowered the rug; now she quickly raises it.*)

> ANYA *is standing behind the rug. She curtseys, runs to her mother and embraces her, then runs back into the ballroom amid general delight.*

RANYEVSKAYA (*applauds*). Bravo, bravo . . .!

CHARLOTTA. Once more, now! *Ein, zwei, drei!* (*Raises the rug.*)

> VARYA *is standing behind the rug. She bows.*

PISHCHIK (*amazed*). Would you believe it!

CHARLOTTA. And that is the end of my show. (*Throws the rug at* PISHCHIK, *curtseys, and runs out into the ballroom.*)

PISHCHICK (*hurries after her*). What a witch, though! What a witch! (*Goes.*)

RANYEVSKAYA. And still no sign of Leonid. I don't understand what he could be doing in town for all this time. It must be over by now. Either the estate is sold, or else the sale never took place. What's the point of keeping us all in suspense?

VARYA (*trying to calm her*). Uncle has bought it – I'm sure of that.

TROFIMOV (*sarcastically*). Oh, of course he has.

VARYA. Great-aunt gave him authority to purchase it in her name, and to transfer the mortgage to her. It was all for Anya's sake. And, God willing, I'm sure Uncle will have done it.

RANYEVSKAYA. To buy this estate – and to buy it in her own name, because she doesn't trust us – your great-aunt sent fifteen thousand rubles – not enough even to pay the interest. (*Covers her face with her hands.*) Today my fate is being decided. My fate . . .

TROFIMOV (*teases* VARYA). Madame Lopakhina!

VARYA (*angrily*). The Wandering Student! They've thrown you out of university twice already.

RANYEVSKAYA. Why are you getting so cross, Varya? All right, he's teasing you about Lopakhin – but what of it? If you want to marry Lopakhin, then marry him. He's a good man, he's an interesting person. If you don't want to, then don't. Darling, no one's forcing you.

VARYA. I must tell you, Mama, that this is something I take very seriously. He's a good man, and I like him.

RANYEVSKAYA. Then marry him. Why wait? I don't understand.

VARYA. Mama dear, *I* can't propose to *him*. For two years now everyone's been talking to me about him. Everyone's been talking except him. He either says nothing or else makes a joke of it. I see why. He's busy making his fortune – he's no time for me. If only we had some money – just a little, a hundred rubles even – I'd throw up everything, I'd go away. I'd go into a nunnery.

TROFIMOV. The glory of it!

VARYA (*to* TROFIMOV). I thought students were supposed to have a little sense in their heads! (*In a gentle voice, with tears in her (eyes.*) Oh, but Petya, you've grown so ugly, you've aged so! (*To* RANYEVSKAYA, *no longer crying.*) It's just that I can't manage without things to do, Mama. Every minute of the day I must have something to do.

Enter YASHA.

YASHA (*scarcely restraining himself from laughing*). Yepikhodov's broken the billiard cue . . .! (*Goes out.*)

VARYA. What's Yepikhodov doing here? Who said he could play billiards? I simply don't understand these people. (*Goes out.*)

RANYEVSKAYA. Don't tease her, Petya. You can see, she's unhappy enough as it is.

TROFIMOV. She's very diligent, I must say that for her. Particularly at minding other people's business. All summer she's given me and Anya no peace. She's been frightened we were going to have some kind of romance. What's it to do with her?

Particularly since I've shown not the slightest sign of it – I'm not given to that sort of vulgarity. We're above such things as love!

RANYEVSKAYA. I suppose I must be beneath them. (*In great anxiety.*) Why isn't Leonid back? If only I knew whether the estate was sold or not. It seems such an incredible disaster that I just can't think – I can't keep control of myself . . . I could scream as I stand here . . . I could do something quite foolish. Save me, Petya. Talk to me about something, talk to me . . .

TROFIMOV. Does it make any difference whether the estate's been sold today or not? All that was finished with long ago – there's no way back – the path's grown over. Be calm now, my dear. Don't deceive yourself. Face up to the truth for once in your life.

RANYEVSKAYA. Yes, but what truth? You can see which is truth and which is falsehood, but I feel as if I'd gone blind – I can't see anything at all. You boldly settle all the great questions, but my love, isn't that because you're young, isn't that because you've never had to live a single one of those questions out? You look boldly forwards, but isn't that because you have the eyes of youth, because life is still hidden from them, so that you see nothing frightening in store? You're more daring than the rest of us, you're deeper, you're more honest – but think about it for a moment, be just a touch magnanimous in your judgment, take pity on me. After all, I was born here, my father and mother lived here, my grandfather . . . I love this house. Without the cherry orchard I can't make sense of my life, and if it really has to be sold, then sell me along with it . . . (*Embraces* TROFIMOV, *and kisses him on the forehead.*) And then this is where my son was drowned . . . (*Weeps.*) You're a good man, a kind man – have pity on me.

TROFIMOV. You know I sympathize with all my heart.

RANYEVSKAYA. Yes, but not said like that, not like that . . . (*Takes out her handkerchief, and a telegram falls on the floor.*)

There is such a weight upon my heart today, you can never know. All this noise here – my heart jumps at every sound – everything in me jumps. But to go away and be on my own – I can't, because as soon as I'm alone and surrounded by silence I'm terrified. Don't judge me, Petya. I love you as if you were my own child. I should have been glad to let you marry Anya – I truly should. Only, my precious boy, you must study, you must finish at university. It's so strange – you do nothing but get yourself tossed by fate from one place to the next. Isn't that true? Yes? And you must do something with your beard somehow to make it grow. (*Laughs.*) You are an absurd man!

TROFIMOV (*picks up the telegram*). I've no desire to be known for my looks.

RANYEVSKAYA. It's a telegram from Paris. Every day they come. One yesterday, another one today. That wild man – he's ill again, he's in trouble again. He begs my forgiveness, he implores me to come, and really I ought to go to Paris, I ought to be with him. You're pulling your stern face, Petya, but my dear, what can I do, what can I possibly do? He's ill, he's lonely and unhappy, and who'll look after him there, who'll keep him from making mistakes, who'll give him his medicine at the right time? And what's the point of hiding it or not talking about it? – I plainly love him. I love him, love him. He's a millstone round my neck – he'll take me to the bottom with him. But I love this millstone of mine – I can't live without it. (*Presses* TROFIMOV's *hand.*) Don't think harsh thoughts, Petya. Don't say anything to me. Don't speak.

TROFIMOV (*on the verge of tears*). Forgive me if I'm frank, please God forgive me, but listen – he's openly robbed you!

RANYEVSKAYA. No, no, no, you mustn't say things like that . . . (*Covers her ears.*)

TROFIMOV. Look, he's no good, and you're the only one who doesn't know it! He's a petty scoundrel, a nobody . . .

RANYEVSKAYA (*angry now, but restraining it*). You're twenty-six, twenty-seven years old, and you're still a schoolboy, you're still a fifth-former.

TROFIMOV. If you say so.

RANYEVSKAYA. It's time you were a man. At your age you must understand people who know what it is to love. You must know what it is yourself! You must fall in love! (*Angrily.*) Yes, yes! You're no more pure than I am! You're just a prig, a ridiculous freak, a monster . . . !

TROFIMOV (*in horror*). What is she saying?

RANYEVSKAYA. 'I'm above such things as love!' You're not above anything – you're merely what our Firs calls a sillybilly. Fancy not having a mistress at your age!

TROFIMOV (*in horror*). This is appalling! What is she saying? (*Rushes towards the ballroom, holding his head.*) Appalling . . . I can't cope with this, I shall have to go . . . (*Goes out, but immediately comes back.*) Everything is finished between us! (*Goes out into the anteroom.*)

RANYEVSKAYA (*calls after him*). Petya, wait! You absurd man! I was joking! Petya!

In the anteroom someone can be heard rushing downstairs, and then suddenly falling with a crash. ANYA *and* VARYA *cry out, but then at once there is a sound of laughter.*

What's happening out there?

ANYA *runs in.*

ANYA (*laughing*). Petya's fallen downstairs! (*Runs out.*)

RANYEVSKAYA. What a freak that Petya is . . .

The STATIONMASTER *takes up a position in the middle of the ballroom.*

STATIONMASTER. The Scarlet Woman. A poem in six parts by Aleksey Konstantinovich Tolstoy. Part One.
> The merry rev'llers throng the hall;
> The lute plays sweet; the cymbals brawl;
> The crystal blazes; gold shines bright;

While 'twixt the columns, rich brocades
Hang swagged with finely broidered braids,
And flowering shrubs anoint the night . . .

People are listening to him, but from the anteroom come the sounds of a waltz, and the reading stops short. Everyone dances. TROFIMOV, ANYA, VARYA *and* RANYEVSKAYA *emerge from the anteroom.*

RANYEVSKAYA. Now, Petya . . . Petya with the pure soul . . . Please forgive me. Shall we dance . . .? (*Dances with him.*)

ANYA *and* VARYA *dance.*

Enter FIRS. *He puts his stick next to the side door.* YASHA *has also entered, and is watching the dancing.*

YASHA. What's up with you, then, Grandad?

FIRS. I'm not right in myself. When we gave a ball in the old days we used to have generals dancing here, we had barons, we had admirals. Now we send for the postmaster and the station-master, and even them they're none too eager. I'm not as strong as I was. The old master, her grandfather, used to treat all our ailments with a dose of sealing-wax. I've been taking sealing-wax every day for twenty years or more. Maybe that's why I'm still alive.

YASHA. Real old bore, aren't you, Grandad? (*Yawns.*) Why don't you just drop dead?

FIRS. Oh, you . . . sillybilly. (*Mumbles.*)

TROFIMOV *and* RANYEVSKAYA *dance first in the ballroom, and then in the drawing-room.*

RANYEVSKAYA. *Merci.* I'm going to sit down for a moment. (*Sits.*) I'm quite tired out.

Enter ANYA.

ANYA (*excitedly*). Some man just came to the kitchen saying the cherry orchard's been sold.

RANYEVSKAYA. Sold? To whom?

ANYA. He didn't say. He's gone now. (*Dances with* TROFIMOV.)

They both go out into the ballroom.

YASHA. That was just some old man gossiping. Some stranger.

FIRS. And Leonid Andreyich still isn't here. He still hasn't come. He's wearing his light autumn coat, he'll go and catch cold. When will these young people learn?

RANYEVSKAYA. I shall die on the spot. Yasha, go and find out who it was sold to.

YASHA. What, from the old man? He left ages ago. (*Laughs.*)

RANYEVSKAYA (*with slight irritation*). What are you laughing at? What are you so pleased about?

YASHA. Very funny man, that Yepikhodov. Fatuous devil. Old Disasters by the Dozen.

RANYEVSKAYA. Firs, if the estate is sold, where will you go?

FIRS. Wherever you tell me to go.

RANYEVSKAYA. Why are you pulling that face? Are you ill? You could go to bed, you know.

FIRS. Oh, yes . . . (*Smiles.*) I go to bed, and who's going to wait on everyone, who's going to see to everything? There's only me to do the whole house.

YASHA (*to* RANYEVSKAYA). Madam, can I ask you a special favour? If you go to Paris again, please take me with you. I can't possibly stay here. (*Looking round and lowering his voice.*) I don't have to tell you – you can see it for yourself. It's an uneducated country, they're people without any morals. And then on top of that there's the boredom – and the food they give us in the kitchen, it's disgusting – and then there's Firs here wandering round all the time muttering away to himself. Take me with you! Please!

Enter PISHCHIK

PISHCHIK. You wonderful woman, may I beg just one thing? One tiny waltz? (RANYEVSKAYA *accompanies him.*) Enchanting creature! All the same, I shall take a hundred and eighty rubles off you . . . I will, you know . . . (*He dances.*) A hundred and eighty tiny rubles . . .

They have passed through into the ballroom.

YASHA (*sings quietly*). 'And will you know just how my heart beats faster . . .?'

In the ballroom a figure in a grey top hat and check trousers waves its arms and leaps about.

VOICES (*off*). It's Charlotta Ivanovna! Bravo!

DUNYASHA (*who has stopped to powder her nose*). Miss told me to dance because there are too many gentlemen and not enough ladies, and now my head's spinning, my heart's pounding. And the postmaster just told me something that quite took my breath away.

The music becomes quieter.

FIRS. What did he tell you?

DUNYASHA. He said, You're like a flower.

YASHA (*yawns*). The ignorance of these people . . . (*Goes out.*)

DUNYASHA. Like a flower . . . I'm such a sensitive girl – I do terribly love it when people say nice things to me.

FIRS. You'll have your head turned, you will.

Enter YEPIKHODOV.

YEPIKHODOV (*to* DUNYASHA). You've no wish to see me, have you . . . As if I was some kind of insect. (*Sighs.*) Ah, life!

DUNYASHA. What do you want?

YEPIKHODOV. And you're right, no doubt, possibly. (*Sighs.*) Though, of course, if you look at it from one point of view, then I mean you have reduced me – and forgive me for saying this, but I mean I'm not going to mince my words – you have reduced me to, well, let's put it like this, to a complete and utter state of mind. I know what's in my stars – every day some disaster happens – I've long been used to it – I look upon my fate now with a smile. I mean, you gave me your word, and although I . . .

DUNYASHA. Please, we'll talk about it later. Leave me in peace now. I'm busy dreaming. (*Plays with a fan.*)

YEPIKHODOV. Every day another disaster, and I mean, all I do is smile. Laugh, even.

Enter VARYA *from the ballroom.*

VARYA (*to* YEPIKHODOV). Are you still here? Have you no respect? (*To* DUNYASHA.) Out of here, Dunyasha. (*To* YEPIKHODOV.) First you play billiards and break the cue, and now you parade about the drawing-room as if you were a guest.

YEPIKHODOV. I'm not going to account for my behaviour to you, if I may say so.

VARYA. I'm not asking you to account for your behaviour. I'm telling you. All you do is wander about from place to place. You never get down to any work. We keep a clerk, but what for, heaven only knows.

YEPIKHODOV (*offended*). Whether I do any work or not – whether I wander about or eat or play billiards – these are questions that can only be judged by people older and wiser than you.

VARYA. You dare to talk to me like that! (*Flaring up.*) You dare! Are you trying to tell me I don't know what's right and wrong? Clear off out of here! This minute!

YEPIKHODOV (*cowering*). Kindly express yourself with more refinement.

VARYA (*beside herself*). Out of here! This instant! Out!

He goes to the door, and she after him.

Disasters by the Dozen – that's right! I want neither sight nor sound of you in here!

YEPIKHODOV *is by now out of the room.*

YEPIKHODOV (*off, behind the door*). I'll tell about you!

VARYA. Oh, coming back, are you? (*Seizes the stick that* FIRS *left beside the door.*) Come on, then . . . Come on . . . Come on . . . I'll show you . . . Are you coming? My word, you're going to be for it . . .! (*Raises the stick threateningly.*)

Enter LOPAKHIN.

LOPAKHIN. Thank you kindly.

VARYA (*angrily and sarcastically*). Sorry! My mistake.

LOPAKHIN. That's all right. I'm touched to get such a warm welcome.

VARYA. Oh, please – think nothing of it. (*Goes away from him, then looks round and asks softly.*) I didn't hurt you, did I?

LOPAKHIN. No, no. Don't worry about it. I shall just have the most enormous bump, that's all.

VOICES (*off, in the ballroom*). Lopakhin's arrived! Lopakhin's here!

Enter PISHCHIK.

PISHCHIK. As large as life . . . (*He and* LOPAKHIN *kiss.*) You smell of brandy, my dear fellow. And we're making merry here as well.

Enter RANYEVSKAYA.

RANYEVSKAYA. Is it him . . .? (*To* LOPAKHIN.) Why so long? Where's Leoníd?

LOPAKHIN. He arrived with me – he's just coming . . .

RANYEVSKAYA (*alarmed*). So what happened? Did they hold the sale? Speak!

LOPAKHIN (*confused, afraid to reveal his joy*). The sale ended just on four o'clock. We missed the train – we had to wait till half-past nine. (*Sighs heavily.*) Ouf! My head's rather going round . . .

Enter GAYEV. *In his left hand he is carrying his purchases; with his right he is wiping away his tears.*

RANYEVSKAYA. Lenya! Lenya!, what happened? (*Impatiently in tears.*) Quickly, for the love of God . . .

GAYEV (*gives her no reply except a flap of the hand; to* FIRS, *weeping*). Here, take these . . . anchovies, Crimean herrings . . . I haven't eaten anything all day . . . Oh, what I've been through!

The door into the billiard room is open; the click of balls can be heard.

YASHA (*off*). Seven and eighteen!

GAYEV's expression changes; he is no longer weeping.

GAYEV. I'm horribly tired. Help me change, will you, Firs? (*Goes off to his room by way of the ballroom, with* FIRS *after him.*)

PISHCHIK. What happened at the sale? Tell us!

RANYEVSKAYA. Is the cherry orchard sold?

LOPAKHIN. It is.

RANYEVSKAYA. Who bought it?

LOPAKHIN. I did.

RANYEVSKAYA is utterly cast down; if she were not standing beside the armchair and the table she would fall. VARYA *takes the keys off her belt, throws them on the floor in the middle of the room, and goes out.*

I bought it! One moment . . . wait . . . if you would, ladies and gentlemen . . . My head's going round and round, I can't speak . . . (*Laughs.*) We got to the sale, and there was Deriganov – I told you he was going to be there. All your brother had was fifteen thousand, and Deriganov straightway bid the mortgage plus thirty. I thought, all right, if that's the way things are, and I got to grips with him – I bid forty. Him – forty-five. Me – fifty-five. So he's going up in fives, I'm going up in tens . . . Well, that was that. I bid the mortgage plus ninety, and there it stayed. So now the cherry orchard is mine! Mine! (*He gives a shout of laughter.*) Great God in heaven – the cherry orchard is mine! Tell me I'm drunk – I'm out of my mind – tell me it's all an illusion . . . (*Stamps his feet up and down.*) Don't laugh at me!

If my father and grandfather could rise from their graves and see it all happening – if they could see me, their Yermolay, their beaten, half-literate Yermolay, who ran barefoot in winter – if they could see this same Yermolay buying the estate . . . The most beautiful thing in the entire world! I have bought the estate where my father and grandfather were slaves, where they weren't allowed even into the kitchens. I'm asleep – I'm imagining it – it's all inside my head . . . (*Picks up the keys, smiling tenderly.*) She threw down the keys – she wants to demonstrate she's no longer mistress here. (*Jingles the keys.*) Well, it makes no odds.

The sound of the band tuning up.

Hey, you in the band! Play away! I want to hear you! Everyone come and watch Yermolay Lopakhin set about the cherry orchard with his axe! Watch the trees come down! Summer cottages, we'll build summer cottages, and our grandchildren and our great-grandchildren will see a new life here . . . Music! Let's have some music!

The music plays. RANYEVSKAYA *has sunk down on to a chair and is weeping bitterly.*

(*Reproachfully.*) Why, why, why didn't you listen to me? My poor dear love, you won't bring it back now. (*In tears.*) Oh, if only it were all over. If only we could somehow change this miserable, muddled life of ours.

PISHCHIK (*takes him by the arm, speaks with lowered voice*). She's crying. We'll go next door and let her be on her own. Come on . . . (*Takes him by the arm and leads him out towards the ballroom.*)

LOPAKHIN. What's all this? Let's hear that band play! Let's have everything the way I want it! (*Ironically.*) Here comes the new landlord, the owner of the cherry orchard! (*Accidentally bangs into an occasional table, and almost overturns the candelabra.*) I can pay for it all! (*Goes out with* PISHCHIK.)

There is no one in either ballroom or drawing-room except
RANYEVSKAYA, *who sits crumpled and weeping bittterly.*
The music plays quietly.

ANYA *and* TROFIMOV *hurry in.* ANYA *goes up to her mother*
and kneels before her. TROFIMOV *remains by the archway into*
the ballroom.

ANYA. Mama . . .! You're crying, Mama? Dear Mama, sweet,
kind, beautiful Mama – I love you and bless you. The cherry
orchard's sold, it's lost and gone – that's true. But don't cry,
Mama. You still have life in front of you. You still have a
generous heart and a pure soul . . . We'll go away, love, you
and me, we'll go away from here, we'll go away. We'll plant a
new orchard, lovelier still, and when you see it you'll
understand. And your heart will be visited by joy, a quiet, deep,
joy like evening sunlight, and you'll smile again; Mama! Come,
love! Come . . .!

CURTAIN

Act Four

The same as Act One.

There are no curtains at the window, and no pictures. A little furniture remains, stacked up in one corner, as if for a sale. You can feel the emptiness.

Upstage, and by the door leading to the outside, are stacked suitcases, bundles made up for a journey, etc.

The door on the left is open, and the voices of VARYA *and* ANYA *can be heard from beyond.* LOPAKHIN *stands waiting.* YASHA *is holding a tray of glasses filled with champagne.*

In the anteroom YEPIKHODOV *is packing a box. From upstage off can be heard a hum of voices – the peasants who have come to say farewell.*

GAYEV (*off*). Thank you, men. Thank you.

YASHA (*to* LOPAKHIN). The peasants have come to make their farewells. They're a decent enough lot, if you want my opinion. They're just not very bright.

The hum of voices dies away.

Enter through the anteroom RANYEVSKAYA *and* GAYEV. *She is not weeping, but she is pale and her face is trembling. She cannot speak.*

GAYEV. Lyuba, you gave them your purse! You mustn't do things like that! You really must not!

RANYEVSKAYA. I couldn't help it! I simply couldn't help it!

They both go out.

LOPAKHIN (*following them to the doorway*). May I humbly

propose a farewell drink? I didn't think to bring any from town, and I could only find one bottle at the station. Come on – have a drink!

Pause.

What – don't you want to? (*Moves away from the door.*) If I'd known I wouldn't have bought it. Well, I shan't have any, either.

YASHA *carefully places the tray on a chair.*

You might as well have a drink yourself, then, Yasha.

YASHA. To all those departing! And to all those staying behind. (*Drinks.*) This isn't real champagne, I can tell you that.

LOPAKHIN. Eight rubles a bottle.

Pause.

Cold as hell in here.

YASHA. They haven't lit the stoves today. Who cares? We're leaving. (*Laughs.*)

LOPAKHIN. What?

YASHA. Sheer pleasure.

LOPAKHIN. October out there, but the sun's shining, the air's still. It's like summer. Good building weather. (*Glances at his watch, and goes to the door.*) Please bear in mind, ladies and gentlemen, you've only forty-six minutes before the train goes! That means we have to leave for the station in twenty minutes. Do make a little haste, now.

Enter TROFIMOV *from outside, wearing an overcoat.*

TROFIMOV. Just about time to go, isn't it? The carriages are here. Heaven knows where my galoshes are. They've vanished. (*Through the doorway.*) Anya, I haven't got my galoshes! I can't find them!

LOPAKHIN. I have to go to Kharkov – I'll be travelling on the same train as the rest of you. That's where I'm staying all winter. I've just been loafing around all this time with you people, going out of my mind with nothing to do. I can't get by without work. I don't know what to do with my hands. They look strange just hanging around like this. They look as if they belonged to somebody else.

TROFIMOV. Well, in a minute we'll be leaving, and you'll be resuming your valuable labours.

LOPAKHIN. Have a glass.

TROFIMOV. I won't, thank you.

LOPAKHIN. So, you're off to Moscow now?

TROFIMOV. Yes, I'm going into town with them. Then tomorrow morning, on to Moscow.

LOPAKHIN. So what, none of the professors been giving their lectures? All waiting for you to arrive, are they?

TROFIMOV. No business of yours.

LOPAKHIN. How many years now have you been at university?

TROFIMOV. Oh, think up something a bit newer than that. That's an old one – old and feeble. (*Looks for his galoshes.*) Listen, we shall probably never see each other again, so allow me to give you one piece of advice as a farewell present. Don't keep waving your arms about! Break yourself of this habit of gesticulating. And all this business of building summer cottages, then calculating that eventually the people who rent them will turn into landlords themselves – that's also a form of arm-waving. All the same, I can't help liking you. You've got fine, sensitive fingers, like an artist's. You've got a fine, sensitive soul, too.

LOPAKHIN (*embraces him*). Goodbye, then, old son. Thanks for everything. Here – just in case you need it – have some money for the journey.

TROFIMOV. What for? I don't need it.

LOPAKHIN. Look, you haven't got any!

TROFIMOV. Yes, I have. Thank you. I got some for a translation I did. Here, in my pocket. (*Anxiously.*) But what I haven't got is my galoshes!

VARYA (*from the next room*). Take your junk away, will you? (*Throws out on to the stage a pair of galoshes.*)

TROFIMOV. Why are you so cross, Varya? Oh, but these aren't my galoshes!

LOPAKHIN. I planted nearly three thousand acres of poppy this spring, and I've made a clear forty thousand rubles on it. But when my poppy was in bloom – what a picture! So here I am, I'm telling you, I've made forty thousand, and I'm offering you a loan because I've got it there to offer. Why turn up your nose? I'm a peasant . . . I'm not going to tie it up in pink ribbon for you.

TROFIMOV. Your father was a peasant, and mine was a dispensing chemist, and from that follows absolutely nothing at all.

    LOPAKHIN *takes out his note-case.*

Leave it, leave it . . . Offer me two hundred thousand if you like, and I still wouldn't take it. I'm a free man. And everything that you all value so highly and dearly – all of you, rich men and beggars alike – it hasn't the slightest power over me. It's just so much thistledown, drifting in the wind. I can manage without you – I can go round the side of you. I'm strong and proud. Mankind is marching towards a higher truth, towards a higher happiness, as high as ever may be on this earth, and I am in its foremost ranks!

LOPAKHIN. And you'll get there, will you?

TROFIMOV. I shall get there.

    Pause.

Either get there, or else show others the way.

    From the distance comes the sound of an axe thudding against a tree.

LOPAKHIN. Well, then, goodbye, old lad. Time to go. We turn up our noses at each other, you and me, but life goes on regardless. When I'm at work – and I can work long hours and never tire – then my thoughts run easier, and I feel I know why I exist. And how many people are there in Russia, my friend, who exist and never know the reason why? Well, it makes no odds –

it doesn't stop the world going round. I'm told her brother's found a job – in a bank, apparently – six thousand a year. Only he'll never stick at it, of course – he's bone idle.

ANYA (*in the doorway*). Mama says will they please not start cutting down the orchard until she's gone.

TROFIMOV. For heaven's sake – how could anyone have so little tact? (*Goes out through the anteroom.*)

LOPAKHIN. I'll see to it, I'll see to it . . . It's quite true – these people . . . (*Goes out after him.*)

ANYA. Has Firs been sent off to the hospital?

YASHA. I told them this morning. I assume they sent him off.

ANYA (*to* YEPIKHODOV, *who is crossing the room*). Ask them, will you, please, if they've taken Firs to the hospital.

YASHA (*offended*). I told Yegor this morning. What's the point of asking ten times over?

YEPIKHODOV. The aged Firs, in my considered opinion, is past repair. It's not a hospital he needs – it's gathering to his fathers. And I can only envy him. (*Puts down the suitcase he is carrying on top of a hat-box, and crushes it.*) Of course! Of course! I knew I was going to do that! (*Goes out.*)

YASHA (*mockingly*). Poor old Disasters!

VARYA (*outside the door*). Have they taken Firs to hospital?

ANYA. Yes, they have.

VARYA. Why didn't they take the letter to the doctor?

ANYA. It'll have to be sent on after him, then. (*Goes out.*)

VARYA (*from the next room*). Where's Yasha? Tell him, will you, his mother's come. She wants to say goodbye to him.

YASHA (*flaps his hand*). Oh, they'll drive me to drink.

DUNYASHA *all this while has been busying herself about things; now that* YASHA *is alone she goes up to him.*

DUNYASHA. If only you'd just give me a glance, Yasha. You're going away . . . abandoning me . . . (*Weeps and throws herself on his neck.*)

YASHA. What's all the crying for? (*Drinks champagne.*) Six days from now I'll be in Paris again. Tomorrow we'll be getting on board that express and we'll be away like smoke. I can't believe it. *Vive la France . . .*! Not my style, this place. I can't live here, there's no help for it. I've seen all I want to see of ignorance – I've had my fill of it. (*Drinks champagne.*) So what's there to cry about? Behave yourself properly, then you won't cry.

DUNYASHA (*powders herself, looking in a little mirror*). You will write to me from Paris, won't you? I loved you, you know, Yasha – I loved you so much! I'm terribly tender-hearted, Yasha!

YASHA. They're coming. (*Busies himself about the suitcases, humming quietly.*)

    Enter RANYEVSKAYA, GAYEV, ANYA *and* CHARLOTTA IVANOVNA.

GAYEV. We ought to be going. We haven't much time in hand. (*Looking at* YASHA.) Who is it smelling of herrings?

RANYEVSKAYA. Another ten minutes, and we'll get into the carriages . . . (*Glances round the room.*) Farewell, dear house. Farewell, old grandfather house. The winter will go by, spring will come, and then soon you won't be here – they'll be pulling you down. So many things these walls have seen! (*Fervently kisses her daughter.*) My treasure, you're radiant – your eyes are sparkling like two diamonds. You're pleased, then? Very pleased?

ANYA. Very pleased. There's a new life beginning, Mama!

GAYEV (*cheerfully*). Absolutely – everything's all right now. Before the cherry orchard was sold we were all frightfully upset, we were all suffering. And then, as soon as the question had been finally settled, and no going back on it, we all calmed down, we got quite cheerful even . . . Here am I, I'm an old hand when it comes to banks – and now I'm a financier . . . yellow into the middle pocket . . . and Lyuba, you look better somehow, you really do.

RANYEVSKAYA. Yes. My nerves are better, it's true.

She is helped into her overcoat and hat.

I'm sleeping well. Take my things out, will you, Yasha. It's time to go. (*To* ANYA.) My own little girl, we'll see each other again soon. When I get to Paris I'll be living on the money your great-aunt in Yaroslavl sent to buy the estate – hurrah for her! But it won't last long.

ANYA. Mama, you'll come back soon, soon . . . won't you? I'm going to study and take my examinations – and then I'm going to work, I'm going to help you. Mama, you and I are going to read all sorts of books together. We will, won't we? (*Kisses her mother's hands.*) We'll read in the autumn evenings, read lots and lots of books, and a marvellous new world will open up before us . . . (*Lost in her dreams.*) Come back, Mama . . .

RANYEVSKAYA. I will, my precious. (*Embraces her.*)

Enter LOPAKHIN. CHARLOTTA *quietly hums a tune.*

GAYEV. Charlotta's happy – she's singing!

CHARLOTTA (*picks up a bundle that looks like a swaddled infant*). My little baby! Off to bye-byes now . . .

INFANT (*cries*). Wah! Wah!

CHARLOTTA. Hush, my pretty one! Hush, my darling boy!

INFANT. Wah! Wah!

CHARLOTTA. Poor little thing! (*Tosses the bundle back where it came from.*) So you'll try to find me a place, will you, please? I can't manage otherwise.

LOPAKHIN. We'll find something for you, never you fear.

GAYEV. They're all leaving us. Varya's going away . . . Suddenly no one needs us any more.

CHARLOTTA. I've nowhere to live in town. I shall have to go farther afield. (*Hums.*) But what do I care?

Enter PISHCHIK.

LOPAKHIN. Well, of all the world's wonders . . . !

PISHCHIK (*out of breath*). Oh, let me get my breath back . . . such a state . . . my dear good people . . . water, some water . . .

GAYEV. After money, is he? No good looking at me . . . I shall depart from temptation. (*Goes out.*)

PISHCHIK. Long time since I was in this house . . . wonderful woman . . . (*To* LOPAKHIN.) And you're here . . . Very pleased to catch you . . . Man of enormous intelligence . . . Here . . . Take this . . . Four hundred rubles . . . Eight hundred still to come . . .

LOPAKHIN (*shrugs in bewilderment*). It's like a dream . . . Where on earth did you get it?

PISHCHIK. Wait . . . Hot . . . Most extraordinary thing. Some Englishmen arrived – found some kind of white clay in my land . . . (*To* RANYEVSKAYA.) And four hundred for you . . . You amazing, wonderful woman . . . (*Gives her the money.*) The rest later. (*Drinks the water.*) Someone was just telling me – young man on the train – apparently there's some great philosopher who recommends jumping off the roof. 'Jump!' he says – and apparently that's the whole problem in life. (*In amazement.*) Would you believe it! Some more water . . .

LOPAKHIN. Who were these Englishmen?

PISHCHIK. I gave them a twenty-four year lease on the section with the clay in it . . . But forgive me, I can't stay now . . . I've got to gallop . . . Go and see old Znoykov . . . And Kardamonov . . . I owe money to all of them . . . (*Drinks.*) Your very good health . . . I'll look in on Thursday . . .

RANYEVSKAYA. We're just moving into town – and tomorrow I'm going abroad.

PISHCHIK. What? (*Alarmed.*) What's this about moving into town? So that's why I can see all this furniture . . . all these suitcases . . . Well, there we are . . . (*On the verge of tears.*) There we are . . . People of the most tremendous intelligence, these Englishmen . . . There we are . . . Be happy . . . God give you strength . . . There we are, then . . . To everything in this world there is an end . . . (*Kisses* RANYEVSKAYA's *hand.*) And if one day the rumour reaches you that the end has come for me, then remember this old . . . this old horse, and say: 'Once on this earth there was a certain Simeonov-Pishchik . . . God rest his soul . . .' Most remarkable weather . . . Yes . . . (*Exits in great confusion, but at once returns and speaks from the doorway.*) Dashenka sends her regards! (*Goes out.*)

RANYEVSKAYA. We could even be going now. I'm leaving with two things still on my mind. One is poor Firs. (*Glances at her watch.*) We could wait another five minutes . . .

ANYA. Mama, Firs has been taken to hospital. Yasha did it this morning.

RANYEVSKAYA. My other worry is Varya. She's used to rising early and doing a day's work. Now she has nothing to do all day she's like a fish out of water. Poor soul, she's grown thin and pale, she's forever weeping . . .

Pause.

(*To* LOPAKHIN.) As you well know, I dreamt of . . . seeing her married to you, and everything appeared to be pointing in that direction. (*Whispers to* ANYA, *who motions to* CHARLOTTA, *whereupon both of them go out.*) She loves you – you like her – and why you seem to avoid each other like this I simply do not know. I don't understand it.

LOPAKHIN. I don't understand it myself, I have to admit. It's all very strange. If there's still time, then I'm ready – here and now, if you like. Let's get it over with, and *basta*. I have a feeling I'll never propose once you've gone.

RANYEVSKAYA. Splendid. It'll only take a minute, after all. I'll call her in at once.

LOPAKHIN. We've even got champagne, appropriately enough. (*Looks at the glasses.*) Empty. Someone's drunk the lot.

YASHA *coughs.*

Well, that really is lapping it up.

RANYEVSKAYA (*animatedly*). Wonderful. We'll go out of the room. Yasha, *allez!* I'll call her . . . (*Through the doorway.*) Varya, leave all that and come here. Come on! (*Goes out with* YASHA.)

LOPAKHIN (*looks at his watch*). Yes . . .

Pause.

There is stifled laughter and whispering outside the door. Finally VARYA *comes in.*

VARYA (*looks round the room at some length*). That's strange. I can't find it anywhere . . .

LOPAKHIN. What are you looking for?

VARYA. I packed it myself and I can't remember where.

Pause.

LOPAKHIN. Where are you off to now, then?

VARYA. Me? To the Ragulins. I've agreed to keep an eye on the running of the house for them. Well, to be housekeeper.

LOPAKHIN. That's in Yashnevo, isn't it? What, about forty-five miles from here?

Pause.

Well, here we are, no more life in this house . . .

VARYA (*examining things*). Where is it . . .? Or perhaps I packed it in the trunk . . . No, no more life in this house. Never again.

LOPAKHIN. And I'm off to Kharkov now . . . on this train, in fact. Lot of business to do. I'm leaving Yepikhodov in charge here. I've taken him on.

VARYA. Really?

LOPAKHIN. This time last year we had snow already, if you remember. Now it's calm and sunny. The only thing is the cold. Three degrees of frost.

VARYA. I didn't look.

Pause.

Anyway, our thermometer's broken . . .

Pause.

A VOICE (*through the door from outside*). Where's Lopakhin?

LOPAKHIN (*as if he has been expecting this call for some time*). Coming! (*Goes rapidly out.*)

VARYA, *now sitting on the floor, lays her head on a bundle of clothing, and sobs quietly. The door opens and* RANYEVSKAYA *cautiously enters.*

RANYEVSKAYA. What?

Pause.

We must go.

VARYA (*she has already stopped crying; wipes her eyes*). Yes, Mama, dear, it's time. I'll get to the Ragulins today provided we don't miss that train . . .

RANYEVSKAYA (*through the doorway*). Anya, get your things on!

Enter ANYA, *followed by* GAYEV *and* CHARLOTTA IVANOVNA. GAYEV *is wearing an overcoat with a hood.*

The SERVANTS *and* CARRIERS *foregather.* YEPIKHODOV *busies himself about the things.*

Well, then, I think we can finally be on our way.

ANYA (*joyfully*). On our way!

GAYEV. My friends! My dear good friends! Leaving this house forever, can I stand silent, can I refrain from saying a word of farewell, from giving expression to those feelings that now invade my whole being . . .?

ANYA (*imploringly*). Uncle!

VARYA. Dear uncle, don't!

GAYEV (*gloomily*). Off the cushion and into the middle . . . I am silent.

Enter TROFIMOV, *followed by* LOPAKHIN.

TROFIMOV. What are we waiting for, then? It's time to go!

LOPAKHIN. Yepikhodov, my coat!

RANYEVSKAYA. I'm going to stop here for one more minute. It's as if I'd never really seen before what the walls in this house were like, what the ceilings were like. And now I look at them avidly, with such a tender love.

GAYEV. I remember, when I was six years old, sitting up on this windowsill on Trinity Sunday and watching my father go to church.

RANYEVSKAYA. Have all the things been taken out?

LOPAKHIN. I think the lot. (*To* YEPIKHODOV, *as he puts on his overcoat.*) Have a look, though, see if everything's all right.

YEPKHODOV (*in a hoarse voice*). Don't worry – leave it to me!

LOPAKHIN. Why are you talking in that sort of voice?

YEPIKHODOV. Just drinking some water, and I swallowed something.

YASHA (*contemptuously*). The ignorance of these people . . .

RANYEVSKAYA. We shall depart, and not a living soul will remain behind.

LOPAKHIN. All the way through until the spring.

VARYA (*pulls an umbrella out of one of the bundles in a way that looks as if she were raising it threateningly:* LOPAKHIN *pretends to be frightened*). What? What are you doing . . .? It never even entered my head.

TROFIMOV. Ladies and gentlemen, we must get into the carriages. It really is time! The train will be arriving any minute!

VARYA. Here they are, Petya – your galoshes, next to this suitcase. (*In tears.*) And what dirty galoshes they are . . .

TROFIMOV (*putting on the galoshes*). Off we go, then!

GAYEV (*in great confusion, afraid of bursting into tears*). The train . . . the station . . . In off into the middle, off the cushion into the corner . . .

RANYEVSKAYA. Off we go!

LOPAKHIN. Are we all here? No one left behind? (*Locks the side door on the left.*) The things are all stacked in here, we must lock up. Right, off we go!

ANYA. Farewell, old house! Farewell, old life!

TROFIMOV. Hail, new life! (*Goes with* ANYA.)

> VARYA *looks round the room and goes out without hurrying.* YASHA *and* CHARLOTTA *go out with her little dog.*

LOPAKHIN. So, until the spring. Out you go, all of you . . . Goodbye! (*Goes out.*)

> RANYEVSKAYA *and* GAYEV *are left alone together. As if they have been waiting for this, they throw themselves on each other's necks and sob quietly, restraining themselves, afraid of being overheard.*

GAYEV (*in despair*). My sister, my sister . . .

RANYEVSKAYA. Oh my dear orchard, my sweet and lovely orchard! My life, my youth, my happiness – farewell! Farewell!

ANYA (*off, calling cheerfully*). Mama!

TROFIMOV (*off, cheerfully and excitedly*). Hulloooo . . . !

RANYEVSKAYA. One last look at the walls . . . the windows . . . This is the room where our poor mother loved to walk . . .

GAYEV. My sister, my sister . . . !

ANYA (*off*). Mama!

TROFIMOV (*off*). Hulloooo . . . !

RANYEVSKAYA. We're coming!

> *They go out.*

> *The stage is empty. There is the sound of all the doors being locked, and then of the carriages departing. It grows quiet. Through the silence comes the dull thudding of the axe. It sounds lonely and sad. Steps are heard.*

> *From the door on the right comes* FIRS. *He is dressed as always, in jacket and white waistcoat, with his feet in slippers. He is ill.*

FIRS (*goes to the door and tries the handle*). Locked. They've gone. (*Sits down on the sofa.*) They've forgotten about me. Well, never mind. I'll just sit here for a bit . . . And I dare say he hasn't put his winter coat on, he's gone off in his autumn coat. (*Sighs anxiously.*) I never looked to see. When will these young people learn? (*Mutters something impossible to catch.*) My life's gone by, and it's just as if I'd never lived at all. (*Lies down.*) I'll lie down for a bit, then . . . No strength, have you? Nothing left. Nothing . . . Oh you . . . sillybilly . . . (*Lies motionless.*)

A sound is heard in the distance, as if from the sky – the sound of a breaking string, dying away, sad.

Silence descends, and the only thing that can be heard, far away in the orchard, is the thudding of the axe.

CURTAIN